CORAL REEFS & ISLANDS

CORAL REEFS & ISLANDS

THE NATURAL HISTORY OF A THREATENED PARADISE

WILLIAM GRAY

Foreword by PROFESSOR DAVID BELLAMY

Technical Editor DR LIAM O'TOOLE

Trustee: Coral Cay Conservation Trust

David & Charles

Designed by Hammond Hammond

Typeset by Goodfellow & Egan Ltd, Cambridge
and printed in Singapore
by CS Graphics Pte Ltd
for David & Charles
Brunel House Newton Abbot Devon

ACKNOWLEDGEMENTS

I am greatly indebted to the many people and
organizations that have been kind enough to
give their help and support in the planning of this
book.

My grateful thanks go to Dr Liam O'Toole, Peter
Raines, Jonathan Ridley and the rest of the Coral
Cay Conservation team, both at the UK office and
the field base on the Belize Barrier Reef; to Dr Ian
Lawn and Ceinwen Edwards at Heron Island
Research Station; to Dr Alec Dawson Shepherd at
the Ministry of Planning and Environment in the
Maldives; to Professor Peter Evans at the
University of Durham and to Professor Jiro
Kikkawa at the University of Queensland. I also
owe my thanks to Dr Mary Stafford Smith of the
Australian Institute for Marine Science; Andrew
Mitchell of Earthwatch; Scarlett Dewar of Friends
of the Earth; Amanda Hillier of the Fauna and
Flora Preservation Society; Martin Robinson and
Don Alcock of the Great Barrier Reef Marine Park
Authority; Barbara Sinclair of the International
Council for Bird Preservation; Jo Taylor of the
World Conservation Monitoring Centre; Gordon
Clark and Dr Elizabeth Wood of the Marine
Conservation Society; Amanda Nicoll of the
Tropical Marine Research Unit (University of
York); Sean Whyte of the Whale and Dolphin
Conservation Society; Andrea Ballard of the
World Wide Fund for Nature; and Rohan Holt,
Simon Zisman and Frank Eckardt.

For invaluable and high-quality support of my
photography during research expeditions, I wish
to thank Jane Harvey of Canon (UK) Ltd; Dawn
Helm of Fuji Photo Film (UK) Ltd; Mike Elsdon of
Paterson Photax Group Ltd; David Darling of Sea
and Sea Ltd; Isabel McCulloch of Colab Ltd; and
G. Armitage of C.Z. Scientific Instruments Ltd. I
am also grateful to Carol Munt of Beaversports Ltd.

Several people have kindly given their advice and
encouragement at each stage of this book's
development. I am particularly grateful to Simon
Gray, Sally Sugg, Vivienne Colvill, Martin
Appleton and my parents; special thanks go to
Sally Littlefield.

CONTENTS

FOREWORD

More than 100,000km (62,000 miles) of the tropical coastlines of the world are or rather were protected by living coral reefs, and tens of thousands of islands and atolls owe their existence to the reef-forming process.

Coral reefs are nature's own front line sea defences, self-building, self-repairing and solar powered, they do the job for nothing and provide homes for more than a third of all the fish species of the world, and a myriad of other sea creatures.

As the sea levels of the world have gone up and down, responding to ice ages and other major upheavals, new reefs have formed, protecting what was left, and growing back to keep the heads of reefs and atolls where they should be, just below the low tide mark. Whilst they grow the reef communities lock up the greenhouse gas, carbon dioxide, into long term store, and as they decay this is released again. Coral reefs are a crucially important part of the life-support systems of Planet Earth.

That was the way of the world less than two hundred years ago, when first the steam and then the petrol engines kick-started destruction on a massive scale.

It has been estimated that damage has been done in 90% of the countries whose coastlines and inshore fisheries are protected by coral reefs, and in 45% of those, that damage is already very serious. For example, of the reefs of Indonesia, the most extensive of any country in the world, only 10% are thought to be in good condition, the rest are dying and in danger of eroding away. The reasons are many: siltation due to forest destruction and land clearance, dredging and mining, pollution, tourist development, overfishing, collecting of marine souvenirs and yes, the fins of snorkellers and scuba divers.

This destruction must stop now, the world needs its coral reefs. I hope that all people from government, through industries large and small, to day trippers, will read this book and learn of the wonders of the coral reefs and islands of our world, before it is too late.

Thank you for caring.

David J. Bellamy
The Conservation Foundation, 1993

David Bellamy, President of Coral Cay Conservation, snorkelling on the Belize Barrier Reef.

OPPOSITE
A colourful variety of marine plants and animals often colonize the under-surface of dead coral skeletons which accumulate in drifts on some reefs.

■

INTRODUCTION

For nearly an hour, the heron had been preening its feathers, stroking its long, slender bill through snowy white plumage that appeared to glow in the late-afternoon sunlight. Occasionally the heron would pause and lift its head. From the high vantage of its roost in one of the island's shoreline trees, it could gaze out across the turquoise lagoon to a distant line of breaking waves, which revealed the position of the coral reef. Beyond this foaming filigree, the shallow reef waters abruptly changed to the dark indigo blue of deep ocean. Seemingly entranced by this spectacular view, the heron became motionless; its head inclined to one side, poised on the graceful curve of a long neck. It was not until the sun had dipped behind the uppermost branches of the island's central forest that the heron stirred again. Other herons were beginning to gather on the beach below, standing hunch-shouldered and silent at the water's edge. The tide was ebbing and the reef-enclosed waters would soon be low enough for the long-legged waders to begin stalking fish through the shallows. The white heron in the shoreline tree momentarily tensed and then leapt from its roost. With wings unfurling to embrace the early-evening breeze, the heron rose into the sky and then banked steeply towards the beach, landing with elegant precision on the coral sand and greeting the other herons with a loud croak.

Long hours of intimate nature watching have been one of the most rewarding and pleasurable aspects of researching this book. Even simple acts of behaviour, like a reef heron taking to flight from its roost, have provided special and memorable experiences. It is often ample satisfaction to wait quietly and just observe, but to capture the essence of a moment, record a striking composition or portray the detailed form of an animal on film or with a sketch is a fascinating challenge.

Coral reefs and islands provide the natural history photographer and artist with a great variety of subjects. During the research for this book, creatures as diverse as fruit bats, moray eels, butterfly fish, crested terns and humpback whales were encountered. In a single day, photographic opportunities could range from a close-up of a timid fiddler crab emerging from

This Caribbean pioneer beach plant produces yellow trumpet-shaped flowers which attract pollinating bees.

OPPOSITE
An adult Pacific, or eastern, reef heron.

Portrait of a pelican; a variety of bird encountered in several coral reef areas.

RIGHT
South Water Cay on the Belize Barrier Reef.

■

its burrow in a mangrove swamp, to a panoramic coral reef seascape, or a bustling sea-bird colony. On a remote island in the South Pacific a long search was rewarded with fleeting glimpses of rare cave swiftlets, while on another island nesting shearwaters were so numerous that it was possible to sketch detailed portraits of them from less than a metre away.

Coral islands are small worlds. The frantic pace at which we so often lead our modern everyday lives must be slowed if the beauty and diversity of their habitats and wildlife are to be fully explored and appreciated. Similarly, the stunning array of life on a coral reef becomes a bewildering procession of colours and shapes unless the time is taken to slow down, pause and look a little while longer.

My aim in writing this book is not to provide a scientific commentary, as research continues and our knowledge constantly changes, but to portray an intimate image of the natural history of coral reefs and islands in order to evoke in the reader an appreciation of their unique beauty and complexity, and an awareness of the importance of conserving this threatened paradise.

Patterned skeletons of coral embedded within beach rock on the shoreline of a coral island.

Dwarf flame angelfish.

■

11

CORAL 1 ISLAND GENESIS

SETTING FOR A CORAL ISLAND

As if each bird had sensed an innate signal, the entire flock of Mongolian plovers took flight. The clattering of their wings and the excited piping of their calls were muffled by a veil of mist that hung heavily over the plain. The lake was already beginning to freeze over and, as the plovers circled one final time over their birthplace, the northerly breeze blew, cold and relentless, with the bitter promise of an Arctic winter. The flock turned towards the south and the annual migration was under way.

Of the millions of wading birds that leave their tundra breeding grounds each year in a frozen grip of ice, thousands head for the sanctuary of coral islands scattered in the warm waters of tropical seas. Similar destinations attract other migrating creatures. Sea turtles ride the swell of ocean currents to reach island beaches where they will lay their eggs, and humpback whales which have journeyed from polar seas give birth to their young in offshore waters.

For a few months of every year, these visitors become part of the complex web of life that makes the coral island one of the richest and most diverse ecosystems on earth. With a beauty comparable to an emerald jewel set in a necklace of turquoise the coral island represents the unique combination of a coral reef and a tiny isolated fragment of tropical land. From steep reef slopes and shallow fields of seagrass, to dense mangrove swamps and sweeping beaches, this ecosystem contains a diverse range of habitats and an impressive array of plants and animals.

Contemplating the existence of rich island worlds thriving in the isolation of vast oceans raises the question of how they form in the first place. Coral island genesis is inextricably linked to the sea where, if a suitable set of conditions is present, a coral reef may begin to grow.

A flock of Mongolian plovers reach the end of their transcontinental migration from eastern Siberia as they skim above the lagoon waters towards their wintering ground on a Great Barrier Reef coral island.

OPPOSITE
A sweeping beach of white sand separates clear reef waters from a dense fringe of coconut palms and shrubs. This scene from Hunting Cay on the Belize Barrier Reef typifies the beauty of a tropical coral island.

Clearly defined against the dark blue of deep ocean waters, a turquoise coral reef grows at a level just below low tide. This particular reef, with its three small coral-sand islands, is part of the Maldive archipelago which stretches for 867km (539 miles) across the Indian Ocean.

GLOBAL DISTRIBUTION OF CORAL REEFS

Coral reefs are found largely between the tropics of Cancer and Capricorn where water temperatures are warm and the climate is sunny all year round. Corals are unable to thrive in water that is much below 16°C (61°F) and grow best within a range of 18–30°C (64–86°F). In the tropics there is little seasonal variation in sea temperature, which suits corals well since they are poorly adapted to fluctuations and would suffer in particularly cool or warm waters.

This is demonstrated very clearly where cold ocean currents penetrate tropical seas. The icy touch of the Benguela Current arching northwards from Antarctic waters inhibits the formation of coral reefs along the west coast of Africa. Where warm currents invade seas beyond tropical latitudes, however, coral reef growth can be maintained. A warm ocean current originating in the Philippines supports coral reefs around southern Japan. The Gulf Stream coursing out of the Caribbean Sea enables

The only place in the world where fur seals and penguins can be found on the Equator is the Galapagos Islands, where the waters are cooled by the Humboldt Current sweeping northwards out of Antarctica.

Sea turtles, such as this green turtle, are often seen in reef waters, particularly during the breeding season when mature adults gather to mate. Females haul themselves into the dunes behind the coral island beaches where they excavate a pit in which to lay their eggs. When the hatchlings emerge, they immediately scramble towards the sea.

■

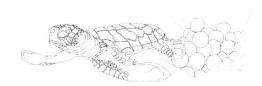

corals to survive in Bermuda, but growth is not vigorous enough to form entire reefs there. The most northerly reef-building corals in the world are to be found in the Red Sea, a narrow enclave surrounded by deserts and warmed by intense solar radiation. In the southern hemisphere warm equatorial currents encourage the coral growth on the Great Barrier Reef to extend beyond the Tropic of Capricorn.

Water temperature is clearly a major controlling factor in the global distribution of coral reefs, but there are many other influences as well. Salinity must be at a favourable level. Freshwater kills coral and this is dramatically illustrated where rivers flow out into coastal reef areas. In addition, the discharge of silt at a river mouth rapidly blankets the delicate and complicated feeding mechanisms of many reef animals including the corals themselves. The River Fly, issuing from the highlands of Papua New Guinea, is responsible for halting the northward progression of the Great Barrier Reef. Similarly, the huge fan of alluvium discharging from the mouth of the River Amazon stops Caribbean reefs colonizing much of the north-east coast of South

Renowned for its dramatic contrast with the surrounding stark desert landscape, the rich, prolific coral growth of the Red Sea forms one of the most extensive reef areas in the world. Fringing reefs thrive on a narrow submerged ledge stretching from the Gulf of Aden northwards to the Gulfs of Suez and Aqaba. The Red Sea reefs often plummet into steep-sided drop-offs reaching several thousand metres in depth. In geological terms, the Red Sea is an 'embryonic ocean', which first developed as a shallow basin at the northern end of Africa's Great Rift Valley, over five million years ago. It has since been growing wider and deeper as sea floor spreading forces Africa and Saudi Arabia further apart. These colossal earth movements have, in the past, caused several reefs to be lifted above the surface. Many of the coral islands in the Dahlak group, Suakin archipelago and at the entrance to the Gulf of Aqaba are raised fossil coral reefs.

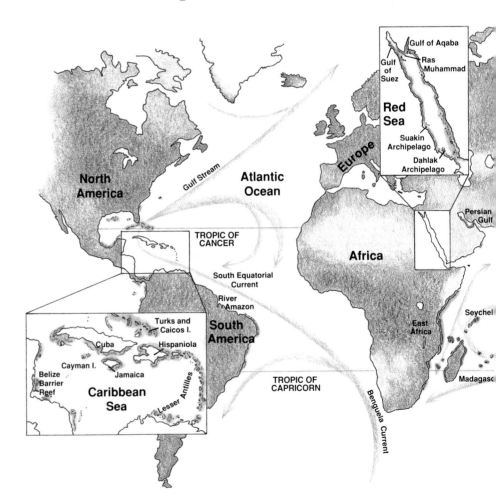

America. However, even established reefs may be threatened by freshwater and silty run-off from neighbouring land during a severe thunderstorm. Such problems are made even worse when agricultural chemicals and other pollutants are allowed to drain into the sea.

A picture emerges, therefore, of coral reefs thriving in an environment with a particular set of conditions controlled by ocean currents, climate and the quality of sea-water. If these were the only factors that determined where reefs could grow it might be expected that a greater proportion of the oceans would contain areas of coral. Viewing a world map, however, reveals a rather scattered distribution, with vast tracts of tropical ocean bathed in warm currents completely devoid of reefs.

To explain this phenomenon requires a closer look at the hidden landscape of the ocean floor. Specialized mapping techniques involving the use of echo sounders and sonars, which measure the strength of returning sound pulses bounced off the sea floor, are used by computers to generate a map of contours. This has effectively enabled us to view the oceans empty of

A variety of plate and branching corals grow in the clear sunlit waters surrounding a Pacific reef.

LEFT
The majority of the world's coral reefs (blue lines) are confined to tropical latitudes. Warm and cold ocean currents (red and blue arrows) play a further role in defining reef distribution, as does the presence of suitable reef foundations. Fresh-water flowing from the mouths of rivers, such as the Amazon and Fly, severely inhibit the growth of reefs.

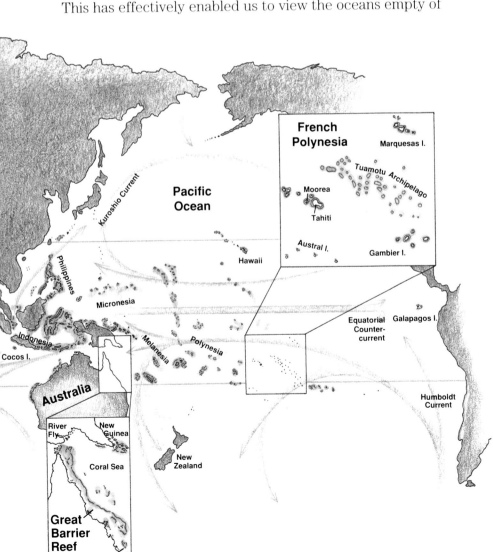

OPPOSITE
A mosaic of small patch reefs pepper the lagoon of a coral atoll in the South Pacific. The only areas of dry land on an atoll are small sandy coral islands which can be seen around the perimeter of this reef.

■

The world-wide distribution of coral reefs is divided into two main realms: the Caribbean, and an area covering both the Indian and Pacific Oceans which is referred to as the Indo-Pacific. Around seventy-five species of reef-building corals are found in the Caribbean, but within the Indo-Pacific this number increases to over three hundred. The Caribbean corals have probably descended from ancient Pacific varieties which could have colonized the region before the Americas were linked by the Panama Isthmus, two million years ago. Floating coral larvae, which disperse in drifting ocean currents in order to reach and colonize other reefs, are unable to survive in the cold waters that sweep around the southern tips of South America and Africa. Consequently, corals in the Caribbean have evolved in isolation from those in the Indo-Pacific.

water and the results have revealed colossal mountain ranges, vast plateaux, plummeting trenches and towering volcanoes. The rugged terrain concealed by the earth's oceans is on a scale unrivalled by anything found on land. If Mount Everest was uprooted and placed on the sea-bed next to the base of Mauna Kea, the Hawaiian volcanic island would rise 1,200m (3,940ft) above the Himalayan peak. Alternatively, Mount Everest could be submerged in the Mariana Trench and still have more than 2,000m (6,560ft) of sea-water covering its summit.

Oceanic mountains, whether they form chains of islands or remain as submerged flat-topped peaks (known as seamounts), perfectly mirror the occurrence of many coral reefs that are found in tropical ocean regions. In addition, there are reefs adjacent to the coastlines of larger continental islands and running alongside continents themselves. Reef-building corals must live in brightly lit waters that are fully penetrated by the sun's rays and this restricts the most luxuriant coral reef growth to depths rarely exceeding 37m (120ft). Beyond this limit too much light is absorbed and in the resulting gloom the life-support systems that nourish the corals cannot be sustained.

Most of the suitably shallow platforms happen to be located in the western tracts of equatorial oceans. In the Atlantic Ocean, most coral reefs are found in the Caribbean Sea. A line equally bisecting the Indian Ocean would group most reefs into the western half, while in the Pacific Ocean there is a huge abundance of coral growth stretching from Indonesia to Polynesia. The reason for this striking pattern is that the geological activity which gives rise to oceanic mountains, broad shallow continental shelves and other favourable platforms for reef growth, is mainly confined to these western regions.

FORMATION OF ATOLLS

The scientists who surveyed the ocean beds discovered that some reefs did arise from submerged foundations at depths considerably greater than 37m (120ft). The atoll reefs of the Maldives, for example, rise from a submarine ridge which lies in nearly 400m (1,310ft) of water. It was perfectly understandable how a coral reef could begin growing in the shallow well-lit waters surrounding an island such as Tahiti in French Polynesia, but how was it that corals could apparently grow towards the surface through several hundred metres of water to reach the critical sunlit layers?

Much research has been carried out in order to find the solution to this mystery. However, all the modern theories that have been proposed are simply developments of an idea one man had more than 150 years ago. The man's name was Charles

The evolution of a coral atoll begins when an underwater volcano emerges as an island above the surface of a tropical sea (A). When volcanic activity ceases, the island begins to erode into a series of jagged peaks and sharp ridges (B) and a fringing coral reef colonizes its shoreline. Erosion, coupled with the buckling of sea floor foundations, strives to return the island below the waves (C); a barrier reef develops as the channel separating it from the island becomes wider and deeper. Eventually, the once mountainous interior of the island is reduced to a low hill (D) and a large lagoon forms inside the reef. When the central island sinks below the surface (E) the reef becomes known as a coral atoll. Low-lying, sandy coral islands (shown in yellow) may begin emerging on the reef at an earlier stage.

■

Hurricanes tracking across the Belize Barrier Reef have wreaked havoc on many of its coral cays. In 1961, Hurricane Hattie obliterated the siricote forest on Half Moon Cay, killing many of the red-footed boobies nesting there. Thirteen years later, Hurricane Fifi swept most of the coconut palms and all other plant life from Carrie Bow Cay. In both places, however, the animal and plant life has recovered.

Darwin and during a five year voyage aboard the survey vessel HMS *Beagle* he became one of the first scientists to investigate the geology and natural history of coral reefs and coral islands. His epic journey took him to the Pacific island of Tahiti as well as the isolated Cocos Islands in the Indian Ocean, and it was there that Darwin envisaged a concept of how reefs developed. He proposed that if an island with a surrounding or fringing reef was to gradually sink, the reef-building corals would maintain upward growth so that even when the highest peak vanished beneath the waves a circular coral reef or atoll would remain flourishing near the surface. Darwin classified the intermediate stage as a barrier reef, when the island had subsided sufficiently to create a lagoon or channel between it and the encircling reef.

On his return to England in 1836 his theory was far too revolutionary to be accepted, but it was confirmed a century

Rarotonga, in the Cook Islands, is an extinct two million year old oceanic volcano. Its crater has long since collapsed to form an impressive island interior of pinnacles and razor-backed ridges that soar to over 650m (2,130ft). A narrow fringing coral reef is well established around the island's shore.

LEFT
Aitutaki, lying 260km (162 miles) north of Rarotonga, is a far older volcanic peak that has been weathered down to little more than 100m (328ft) above sea-level. Its coral reef surrounds a large lagoon.

■

later when two boreholes drilled into Enewetak Atoll in the Marshall Islands reached volcanic rock after passing through well over 1,000m (3,280ft) of coral limestone. This proved that a central volcanic core had originally been near enough to the surface to allow coral reefs to begin growing around it. As it subsided the reef corals continued to deposit a limestone skeleton to ensure they remained near the surface where sufficient sunlight could maintain their growth.

Throughout the world there are numerous places where Darwin's theory of atoll evolution can be applied. The seventy-five atolls of the Tuamotu Group in French Polynesia, for example, crown the drowned summits of a huge ridge which millions of years ago would have pierced the surface of the Pacific as a spectacular volcanic island chain.

One of the main criticisms of Darwin's new theory was the unacceptable view that whole islands could rise and sink. Darwin did not have the sophisticated means to produce the kind of evidence that present-day geologists have at their disposal, but he was nevertheless aware that subterranean forces were involved. Today, we refer to these 'forces' in terms of plate tectonics, and understand far more about the ways in which they can create and destroy islands than even Darwin could have predicted.

The ocean floors act rather like giant conveyor belts, spreading away, millimetre by millimetre, from ocean ridges. Each fresh extrusion of molten basalt from the ridge fuels the process and in a single year up to 10cm (4in) of new ocean floor can be produced. Such movements may seem imperceptible, but they have the power not only to carry continents into collision with each other, but also to force them apart. The Atlantic Ocean was non-existent two hundred million years ago. The Americas were fused with Africa and Europe into a great 'supercontinent' known as Pangaea. When dinosaurs were in their prime Pangaea began to fragment, each piece drifting away like a leaf borne on the spreading ripples of a pond. The new Atlantic cleaved Pangaea in two, and North and South America began to drift into the west as fresh sea floor was forged at the mid-ocean ridge.

When the leading edges of spreading ocean floors encounter resistance they are deflected downwards and remelted in the earth's mantle before being violently spewed to the surface again through volcanoes. The volcanic island chains around the edge of the Pacific, aptly named the Ring of Fire, are derived in this way as are the Lesser Antilles of the Caribbean. Island chains such as Hawaii which rise in the centre of the Pacific Ocean are formed by a slightly different process, but one which still relies on the slow spreading of the sea floor.

A soft glow of pre-dawn light silhouettes fragments of basalt littering the shoreline of a volcanic island while, in the distance, waves break across a fringing reef with the continuous sound of muted thunder.

■

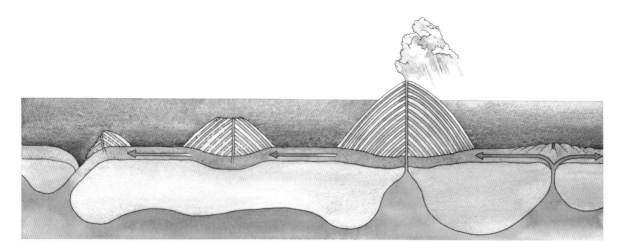

Seventy kilometres (43 miles) below the giant smouldering craters of Mauna Loa and her less active sister Mauna Kea on the island of Hawaii lies a 'hot spot' – a particularly volatile concentration of seething magma in the earth's upper mantle. The intense heat generated within the hot spot causes bubbles of molten rock to rise upwards and as each pulse reaches the surface Mauna Loa erupts. Scarlet rivers of lava streak her blistered slopes and then harden to basalt amidst furious clouds of steam as the flows enter the sea. Each new eruption nourishes the island, feeding it raw rock and building its summit ever higher above the Pacific; 700,000 years ago the island of Hawaii was simply a small volcanic cone pimpling the floor of the ocean. As it grows and ages, the frequency of volcanic eruptions will dwindle and finally stop altogether. Eventually the steadily moving sea floor will carry Hawaii away, severing its link with the hot spot. In fact, a new submarine volcano called Loihi is already forming on the seabed south of Hawaii.

In this part of the Pacific the ocean floor is spreading in a north-west direction, carrying the Hawaiian Islands to their fate within the destructive depths of the Aleutian Trench. As each young volcanic island begins this seventy million year ocean crossing it undergoes a series of changes. Its soaring peaks, deprived of their magma supply, are at the mercy of crashing waves and scouring wind and rain. The forces of erosion, coupled with the buckling and subsidence of sea floor foundations as they struggle to support the towering mass of the volcanic peak, endlessly strive to return the island beneath the sea. Before the sea lays final claim, however, a fringing coral reef begins to flourish on the submerged flanks of the island. Just as Darwin proposed, the corals maintain upward growth and even after the island volcano has been reduced to a submerged seamount an atoll reef remains near the surface – a turquoise wreath of coral laid down in the image of a vanished island shore.

This entire sequence is demonstrated by the Hawaiian Islands. Midway and Kure Atolls are founded on ancient seamounts that have been carried 2,250km (1,400 miles) north-west from Hawaii during the past twenty-seven million years.

The life and death of a volcanic island is portrayed in this illustration. New sea floor is created at an ocean ridge (*right*) and carries an island volcano away from its 'hot spot' magma source to be destroyed in an ocean trench (*left*).

■

Encircling the northern and western rims of the Pacific Ocean is a chain of volcanic islands. The Ring of Fire, as it is known, enters the tropical latitudes of the Pacific at the Mariana Islands before snaking eastwards across the top of New Guinea and then looping through the Solomon Islands, Vanuatu and Fiji. Another volcanically active chain of islands stretches south from Samoa, passing through Tonga before finally ending in New Zealand's fiery North Island. Many of the tropical islands in the Ring of Fire have extensive coral reef formations. The Solomon Islands include large atolls such as Ontong Java which has a lagoon of 1,400 square kilometres (540 square miles). The Great Astrolabe Reef and the 200km (125 miles) long Great Sea Reef flourish in the seas around Fiji.

The Capricorn Group lies at the southern end of the Great Barrier Reef and is made up of a cluster of platform reefs, many of which have low coral islands. Here, a deep-water channel separates Heron and Wistari Reefs.

■

Nearly all tropical oceanic islands with their associated fringing and barrier reefs, together with seamounts and coral atolls, result from volcanic activity.

THE GREAT BARRIER REEF

Some of the greatest coral reef structures on earth do not conform so easily to Darwin's explanation. The straightforward progression from fringing to barrier and then atoll reefs, for example, cannot be responsible for the complex pattern of different shaped reefs that comprise the Great Barrier Reef. Covering an area larger than Great Britain and half the size of Texas, the Great Barrier Reef is composed of more than 2,600 individual reefs extending along 2,300km (1,430 miles) of Queensland's coastline from the Gulf of Papua to just beyond the Tropic of Capricorn.

It was not until two million years ago that Queensland reached the Tropic of Capricorn, pushed by the colossal forces of continental drift that are still ponderously advancing Australia's northward journey. At that time the sea level was much lower than it is today due to a massive volume becoming locked into the ice-cap that was forming over Antarctica. When this ice age ended, the sea levels started to rise again and in the shallow warm waters that flooded the continental shelf off Queensland, the Great Barrier Reef began to grow.

The reason for the sudden growth of corals is unknown, but it is likely that a rapid rise in sea level washed the mud and silt from the continental shelf to produce clear shallow water conditions, favourable to corals' colonization. The first reefs began to flourish on the stable banks and islands of former rivers which were being drowned by the swelling waters of the transgressing ocean. The advancing sea stranded several small hills, cutting them off from the mainland and isolating them as continental islands. Many, such as the Whitsunday Islands, developed fringing reefs around their shores.

Just over 100,000 years ago, disaster befell this particular version of the Great Barrier Reef. A new ice age had started and, once more, the seas began to recede. The coral reefs were exposed permanently to air and then eroded by wind and rain. Rivers from the Great Dividing Range of Australia flowed out across the vast plain of the uncovered continental shelf and gashed gorges through the limestone cliffs that had once formed the base of the Great Barrier Reef.

There is an ancient myth in the Aboriginal Dreamtime that describes a journey of their people across a flat plateau with wide rivers that flowed to a white escarpment on the horizon. Man has never again been able to walk from Australia to the Great Barrier

The Great Barrier Reef is an assortment of many different reefs which lie at various distances from the Queensland coast of Australia. This reef is one of the closest, lying only 27km (17 miles) from the towering Atherton Tablelands near Cairns.

■

Reef. Eight thousand years ago the Second Ice Age ended and sea once more flooded the continental shelf, drowning the footprints of the Aborigines' remarkable journey.

The Great Barrier Reef began to grow again. Keeping pace with rising sea levels it built its groundwork on the ancient remains of the first barrier reef. In some regions river erosion during the period of low sea level had severely disrupted the outlines of the old foundations. Fresh coral growth during the last several thousand years has faithfully reproduced the images of vanished rivers, creating meandering paths of deep channels which today separate entire reefs. Flying over the Pompey Reef Complex, it is possible to make out the prehistoric river courses that had eroded gorges through the reef during the Second Ice Age.

The shapes of modern reefs are, therefore, largely inherited from the shapes of earlier ones that have been modified by erosion during periods of low sea level. Oceanographic factors such as the strength of ocean currents have also played a role in shaping the Great Barrier Reef. The long sinuous ribbon reefs found in the northern reaches are strongly influenced by the sculpturing surge of water movements.

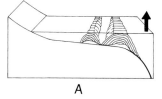

A

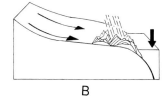

B

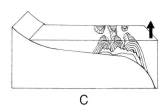

C

The growth of the Great Barrier Reef has been greatly influenced by fluctuations in sea level caused by ice ages. Reefs began to grow on Australia's continental shelf two million years ago when melting ice caps raised the level of the oceans (A). During a subsequent ice age the sea level dropped, exposing the reefs to river erosion and weathering (B). When sea levels were restored after the ice age, renewed coral reef growth mirrored the shapes of the eroded foundations (C).

■

ARCHITECTS OF THE REEF

The bare rocky shores of a newly erupted volcanic island present a hostile challenge for the reef-building corals that attempt to colonize them. The first problem facing a coral is how to reach the unclaimed coastline, which may be many hundreds of miles away from the nearest reef. Even after this is accomplished, how does the coral succeed in attaching itself and then grow to form entire reefs that can withstand pounding waves at low tide and even keep pace with sinking land masses or rising sea levels? In contrast to the high production of plankton and nutrients in cold polar seas, most of the tropical regions of open ocean are as barren as watery deserts. The Atlantic South Equatorial Current, for example, is fed mainly by the plankton-rich upwellings of the cold Benguela Current, but most of its nutrient content has been eaten or has died by the time it reaches the tropical Caribbean. How then do corals find enough food to sustain their growth?

Modern reef-building corals have developed perfect lifestyles to cope with these environmental problems since they started evolving in the Tertiary Period, some twenty-five million years ago.

A tiny animal called a polyp, resembling a miniature sea anemone with a soft sac-shaped body which opens at one end into a mouth surrounded by tentacles, first appeared in primeval

Reef-building corals flourish at the crest of an Indian Ocean reef. The complex intricacy of shapes on a reef seems even more bewildering when calm seas produce a mirror image reflection at the surface.

seas over half a billion years ago, and today the same type of creature forms the basic unit for all corals.

In most corals, each polyp nestles within the protective walls of a limestone cup which it secretes using the calcium carbonate dissolved in sea-water. Polyps can reproduce asexually, producing identical daughter polyps by a process known as budding. As each new polyp is added, another limestone cup is secreted under and around it, helping to build a supporting framework for the entire colony, and in this way a coral can grow outwards and upwards. A single polyp of *Porites* coral measuring only 1mm (0.04in) in diameter is capable of budding and depositing limestone to form a massive boulder-shaped colony over 10m (33ft) across. The ability of corals to duplicate themselves in this prolific manner and lay down considerable thicknesses of rock are major factors enabling reefs to develop. Different types of coral bud in different ways and this leads to the incredible variety of shapes present on a coral reef.

Budding may help solve the problem of reef building, but it does not explain how corals can colonize remote shorelines in the first place. To do this corals turn to sexual reproduction, releasing eggs and sperms which when fused develop into tiny free-floating larvae called planulae. The larvae can then be

The polyps of the hard coral *Goniopora* remain extended at all times and may reach several centimetres in length. A small mouth is visible at the centre of each ring of tentacles.

BELOW
A small piece of coral rock clearly shows the limestone skeleton that the polyps deposit to enable them to grow upwards and outwards. This fragment was eroded from a reef before becoming cemented into a band of beach rock along the north coast of Rarotonga in the South Pacific.

ABOVE AND LEFT
Corals grow in a wide variety of shapes. A brain coral *(left)* has a convoluted pattern with rows of polyps separated by a ramifying network of walls, while an *Astraea* coral *(right)* produces a quite different pattern.

■

A close-up view of coral sand reveals the detail of its composition. Much of the material shown here consists of ground fragments of coral and broken shell; a reflection of the erosive action of particularly strong waves that crash against the nearby reef.

■

carried across wide stretches of ocean and if currents are favourable enough to brush against a shallow tropical shoreline, the planulae swim downwards and locate a suitable spot on which to transform themselves into coral polyps. The minute and vulnerable polyps rapidly secrete calcareous skeletons and the process of building a new colony begins.

The rate at which coral polyps grow and create their skeletons is greatly increased by the remarkable association with a plant which actually lives within the animal tissues of each polyp. The plant is a single-celled alga called zooxanthellae and this intimate relationship is referred to as a symbiosis because both host animal and lodging plant receive benefit from the arrangement. The precise situation is complex, but the algae are thought to induce the polyp to secrete its limestone skeleton which, in turn, provides a protected and stable environment for the plant cells to live in. However, the relationship does not end there. An intriguing exchange system takes place which not only provides food for both plant and animal components, but also solves the problem of how reefs are able to flourish in tropical seas so poorly endowed with nutrients. The energy of the sun's rays is captured inside each algal cell and is used to power the splitting of carbon dioxide and water which then recombine as oxygen and carbohydrate. This process is called photosynthesis and it is one of the most fundamental reactions enabling the earth to sustain life.

The animal tissues of the polyp use as much as 80% of the carbohydrate food produced by the algae to fuel their growth and metabolism. The algae require the remaining starchy compounds for their own maintenance but, like all plants, they must also have nitrogen and phosphorus to survive. These minerals are in very short supply in tropical waters, but by teaming up with the polyps the zooxanthellae algae have a guaranteed supply. Ammonia, which contains these essential minerals, is a natural waste product of the coral polyp. Rather than ejecting it as most animals do, the ammonia is stored and then absorbed by the algae. Once inside the plant tissue it is modified and built into proteins which can be used by both polyp and algae.

This intimate collaboration between animal and plant results in a highly efficient self-contained life-support system for which the only essential raw materials are sunlight and carbon dioxide, both of which are abundant in shallow tropical seas. All nutrients and precious minerals are carefully recycled both within the polyps themselves and by a multitude of other plants and creatures that inhabit the reef.

Although polyps also feed externally by catching plankton

This limestone boulder of a dead coral colony has become carpeted with a thin felt of green algae. It is frequented by herbivorous parrotfish and surgeonfish which leave bare scars where they rasp away the algae with their teeth.

OPPOSITE
Surgeonfish and tangs gather into a large feeding shoal, browsing their way along the towering wall of a reef slope in the northern reaches of the Great Barrier Reef.

■

A prolific growth of *Halimeda* algae forms a backdrop to a variety of diverse reef fish. From top left to bottom right are juvenile clown wrasse, three-striped humbug damselfish, bi-colour dottyback, juvenile koran angelfish, copper-banded butterfly fish and lionfish. A well-camouflaged abalone snail browses on the algae behind the butterfly fish.

■

or suspended particles (such as dead fragments of animals or their floating eggs and larvae) that drift within range of their stinging tentacles, this may only meet 10% of their total energy requirements. It is the symbiotic algae within their tissues that allow corals to build entire reefs.

Reef-building corals obviously rely on the benefits their lodgers provide since they only grow in shallow water where sunlight can be fully harnessed for photosynthesis. The image of a coral reef as a massive aggregation of thriving animal colonies is true but deceptive, since it is the hidden exploits of plants that dominate and control its activities.

REEF BUILDING

If a reef was simply a disjointed collection of corals growing around and on top of each other it would soon succumb to the ravaging power of surging currents, tropical storms and the pounding waves of low tide. In reality, coral reefs are carefully engineered structures built and shaped by the activities of a wide range of plants and animals and by the indirect influences of the surrounding sea.

Individual coral colonies provide the raw building blocks for a reef, but like any large construction a matrix or cement is required to strengthen and hold it together as it increases in size. The ingredient of this 'reef mortar' is coral sand. A dynamic relationship exists whereby new coral growth constantly replaces fragments broken off by waves at the reef crest or dislodged by currents further down the reef slope. The soft living tissue of the coral polyps often disintegrates in the process, but the hard resistant limestone skeletons enter a cycle of attrition where continued battering and abrasion gradually reduces them to fine particles of coral sand. The empty shells of bivalves and gastropods are also broken up by waves and enter the sand cycle, adding a subtle range of pink and yellow hues to the end product.

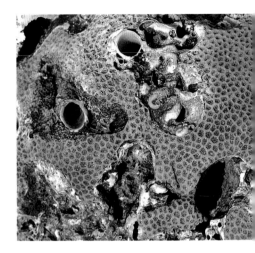

Burrowing worms are one of the most destructive of all reef-dwelling creatures, as this partially obliterated coral demonstrates.

In addition to this direct form of erosion, the reef faces a daily onslaught from several of its inhabitants. Large mixed shoals of herbivorous fish can often be seen moving across the reef in a writhing mass of dancing tails and bobbing heads as they browse on a thin turf of green algae. Parrotfish, surgeonfish and tangs use their strong beak-like teeth to rasp away the algae, but as the clicking crunching sounds of a feeding shoal testify, a large amount of coral rock is also bitten off. The vegetarian fish sieve each gritty mouthful for its plant content and then jettison the unwanted material as a cloud of instant sand through their gills. The large titan triggerfish, common in the Maldives, uses its powerful jaws to pulverize shellfish against coral boulders, rather like a thrush uses a rock as an anvil against which to break the shells of snails. For every soft body that is extracted and eaten, a hard shell is abandoned and shattered into tiny fragments.

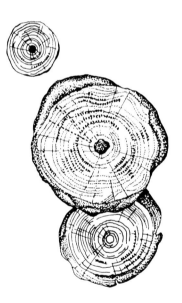

These Foraminiferan skeletons are less than 5mm (0.20in) in diameter, and at some locations they form a significant part of coral sand.

Worms which bore tunnels through corals are another major contributor of sand. Using acidic secretions to dissolve the limestone skeleton, or by mechanical grinding, these animals can create an extensive ramifying system of tubes within the coral. Burrowing worms are surprisingly abundant within the reef structure. A small dead coral head from Heron Island on the Great Barrier Reef was found to contain 1,441 individual boring worms from more than one hundred species.

Algae also contribute to the vast quantities of sand produced on the reef, and may produce more than the coral itself. One family, known as Halimeda, actually deposit granules of calcium carbonate inside their leafy disc-shaped fronds. When an algal disc dies, the surrounding plant tissue decays leaving only grains of sand.

Other significant producers of coral sand particles are the Foraminiferans, an order of single-celled animals which, like many of the corals, have enrolled symbiotic algae to help them flourish in tropical waters. Most Foraminiferans are microscopic, but some may reach over a centimetre in diameter, depositing a circular calcareous disc as they grow. Their skeletal remains are destined to become yet another ingredient of coral sand.

Some of this sand is washed away in ocean currents and a large quantity accumulates on the shoreward side of fringing and barrier reefs or within the central lagoon of atolls and smaller elliptical platform reefs. The build-up of sediment on the leeward side of a reef plays a vital role in the formation of sandy coral islands, as will become clear in a later section.

A large proportion of the sand, however, becomes trapped in crevices and holes within the reef itself, infilling spaces between coral colonies and patching up areas damaged by storms. As these deposits form they are cemented in place by an alga which grows in a very unusual manner. Encrusting coralline algae have the appearance and texture of a smooth pink rock and, indeed, up to 95% of the plant is composed of limestone. The remaining 5% of living plant tissue deposits solid calcium carbonate in hard films across most of the 'dead' surfaces found on a reef.

The polyps of this staghorn coral are extended during the night when the animal feeds on floating plankton. Two small daughter polyps have begun to grow as 'buds' from the sides of the larger polyps.

■

Several thousand islands occur within the tropical zones of the Atlantic, Indian and Pacific Oceans, and the majority of them have close links with coral reefs. Some, such as the Maldives, Tuamotus and Marshall Islands, are low-lying cays built from coral sand. The Rock Islands of Palau, several islands in the Solomon and Cook groups as well as Aldabra Atoll are raised coral reefs. The volcanic islands of the Lesser Antilles, together with the high islands of the Pacific such as Tahiti in the Society Group and parts of Hawaii, Fiji, and Tonga all have surrounding coral reefs.

■

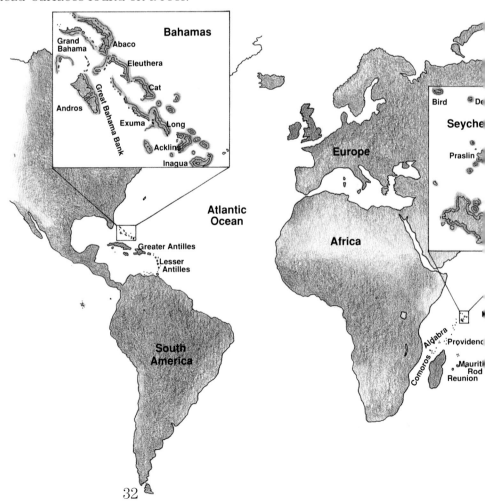

Dead coral skeletons are now being used by some American surgeons for bone-graft operations, eliminating the need to remove natural bone from other areas of the body.

Encrusting algae act as a perfect cement, consolidating the entire framework of the reef. In areas where even the hardiest of corals cannot survive the relentless pressure of breaking waves, such as on a particularly exposed reef crest, pink encrusting algae will dominate, ensuring the stabilization of the reef in this critical zone known as the algal rim. In fact, these unusual plants seem actually to benefit from the constant crashing impact of breakers.

As the limestone superstructure of the reef is strengthened by pockets of sand and cementing algae, another design feature evolves which aims to reduce the impact of waves before they reach the main slope of the reef. A system of spurs and grooves, resembling the battlements and fortifications of a castle wall, grows out from the reef slope. No one knows exactly how the spurs are formed, but it seems likely that ridges of algal-cemented coral slowly build out for several metres into the sea, creating narrow gullies or grooves between adjacent spurs. The backwash of a spent wave is naturally channelled into the gullies and collides with the next oncoming wave with such force that its full power is shattered before it can be unleashed directly onto the reef slope. Spur and groove systems are most highly developed on sections of reef which receive the brunt of ocean swells.

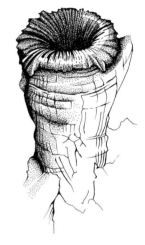

ABOVE
A 400 million year old fossil coral (*Ketophyllum*) preserved in limestone from the Wenlock Ridge in Shropshire, England.

■

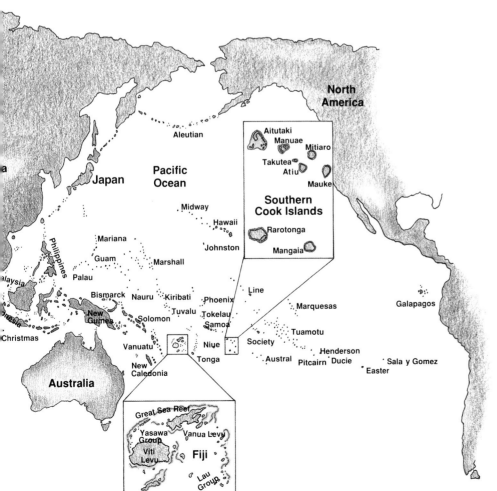

More than eleven million years ago the Pacific island of Atiu, lying in the Cook group, emerged above the surface as a young volcanic island. Over the aeons, the towering peak was eroded to a low-lying shoal of volcanic sediment and in the surrounding waters an extensive coral reef developed. Then, one hundred thousand years ago, the oceanic foundations of Atiu had a series of convulsions which heaved both the island and its reef 20m (65ft) out of the sea. The coral reef became a flat, 1km (1,100yd) wide, coastal plain and was soon cloaked with dense jungle. Today, as this view shows, a new fringing reef has started growing in the waters below the vertical cliffs of the raised fossil reef.

■

The whole process of reef building is a slow one. Over a period of perhaps a million years it can ensure the strength and stability of an oceanic atoll built up from a platform lying a kilometre below the surface, or, as in the Great Barrier Reef, create the only structure built by living creatures that is visible from space. All this seems even more remarkable when one contemplates the creature ultimately responsible: a coral polyp measuring 10mm (0.40in).

CORAL ISLANDS OF THE WORLD

There are many types of coral islands scattered throughout the world's tropical seas where reefs flourish but only one or two varieties can be truly classed as 'islands of coral'.

One of these, the so-called 'raised reef islands', is a rare and special case created by the upheaval of entire reefs. Such catastrophic uplift is usually related to volcanic activity forcing the reef's foundation upwards. Sometimes a lowering in sea level may have a similar stranding effect. Once marooned the reef dies to leave a flat and barren island which often weathers into a jagged relief pitted with caves and sinkholes. On the raised islands of Atiu and Mauke in the Cook Islands there are extensive cavern systems dripping with stalactites.

The perimeter of a raised reef island is defined by short vertical cliffs of limestone in which the fossilized skeletons of reef-building corals can be seen. Very often a fringing reef will begin to grow close offshore, but if conditions are still unstable this too may be uplifted, creating a stepped series of stranded reefs.

One of the most spectacular raised coral islands in the world is Aldabra Atoll in the Indian Ocean. Strange mushroom-shaped pinnacles of fossil coral dot Aldabra's swampy lagoon, owing their shape to the undercutting action of waves. In western Micronesia, a whole chain of raised reefs, known as the Rock Islands, have been eroded in a similar way.

The other true coral islands are made entirely of sand or shingle. They are the by-products of the coral reef, disgorged and then nourished by a huge range of sand and debris producing activities that take place on the reef. This type of coral island is often referred to as a 'coral cay'. The ring-shaped reef of an atoll may form a necklace of coral cays (known as *motus* in the Pacific) around the perimeter of its lagoon.

The twenty-nine large atolls of the Pacific Marshall Islands have given rise to over 1,000 motus. Lying within this group is Kwajalein Atoll which is the largest in the world, enclosing a central lagoon some 2,200 square kilometres (850 square miles) in area. Despite its colossal size, the coral islands of Kwajalein

Erskine Island is a small coral cay crowning one of the reefs in the Capricorn Group of the Great Barrier Reef.

■

34

barely constitute 16 square kilometres (6 square miles) of dry land. Likewise, the entire Maldive archipelago off the south-western tip of India shares its 300 square kilometres (116 square miles) of land between 1,300 islands. Only nine are larger than 2 square kilometres (0.75 of a square mile).

The 261 atolls of the world are not the only reef platforms that can support these low sandy coral islands. A wide range of reef types on both the Great Barrier Reef and the Belize Barrier Reef, for example, has given rise to hundreds of coral cays. The complicated barrier and fringing reef systems around Fiji include over two hundred cays while north of Java, at the Kepulauan Seribu Reserve, lies a group of reefs with more than a hundred low coral islands.

The total absence of any volcanic or continental rocks clearly distinguishes these low-lying sandy islands from the larger 'high coral islands'. The South Pacific volcanic islands of Tahiti, Fiji and Rarotonga typify the majestic beauty of this variety of coral island, with their central interiors of towering razor-backed ridges surrounded by narrow coastal plains. Submarine volcanoes emerging as islands in the warm waters of tropical seas are often colonized by fringing reefs, and as a result of this association they are termed high coral islands. Apart from

providing the materials for a white coral-sand beach, the fringing reef does not contribute to the construction of the island.

Similarly, continental islands are always formed first and then encircled by the turquoise ring of a coral reef at a later stage. Continental islands are of two types. The majority, including many of the Indonesian archipelagoes, as well as the islands lying close to the Queensland coast of Australia, have been created after rising sea levels have isolated them from the neighbouring mainland. The Seychelles and parts of New Caledonia on the other hand, are located in mid-oceanic regions and represent the discarded chunks of ancient continents. The giant rounded boulders of pink granite, which lie scattered on many beaches in the Seychelles, betray their ancestry to a continent which millions of years ago drifted apart and isolated these islands in the middle of the Indian Ocean.

The high islands in the Caribbean Sea, many of which are fringed with coral reefs, demonstrate a wide range of origins. Cuba, Hispaniola, Jamaica and Puerto Rico are all ancient volcanic islands which have been heavily weathered. The Lesser Antilles are also largely volcanic but more recent in age. Barbados, however, is composed of a giant slab of limestone which crowns the highest summit of a submarine mountain ridge extending north from South America.

The Bahamas, lying at the northern limits of the Caribbean Sea, also have a fascinating origin. This is the only open-ocean island system lying within the tropics of the Atlantic and consists of a mixture of 2,750 low-lying continental islands, coral cays and rocky outcrops. Two million years ago the whole region used to be a desert with rolling sand dunes, but at the end of the last ice age when sea levels began rising around the world this landscape was flooded. Many Bahaman islands such as Acklins Island represent the fossilized dune ridges of the prehistoric desert and in the surrounding shallow seas coral reef growth is now prolific.

THE REEF-BORN ISLES

To encounter islands made from sand lying no more than five metres above sea level in the midst of unbroken ocean horizons is to witness one of nature's greatest achievements, for it is the living and growing coral reef that creates these terrestrial oases.

Corals are marine creatures and the reefs they build are therefore restricted to a level just below low tide. How then can they be responsible for producing islands which rise several metres above water? The whole process of building these true coral islands revolves around the timeless struggle for supremacy between land and sea. To begin with, the battle is fought solely beneath the surface.

INDIAN OCEAN

The coral atolls of the Maldives are home to a variety of sea-birds including Audubon's shearwater (*top*), white-tailed tropicbird (*middle*) and least frigatebird (*bottom*). The dominant vegetation on the atoll's low sandy coral islands is the coconut palm.

■

Once a reef begins growing in shallow sunlit waters it invites the relentless onslaught of breaking waves. A coral reef can be identified anywhere in the world simply by the foaming filigree of crashing waves around its edge. Piece by piece the reef is shattered and eroded by the battering impact of the sea. New coral growth, however, is also a continuous process. Corals which are plucked away during storms provide a vacant site on the reef for a new colony to start growing on. Sometimes during a cyclone or hurricane the surface is whipped into such a fury that chunks of reef the size of houses are torn away. After such freak storms the reef may take several decades to recover fully.

The dynamic processes of continuous erosion and vigorous coral growth result in the production of huge quantities of reef debris. Dome-shaped boulders of brain coral skeletons, shattered antlers of staghorn corals and the broken flat discs of plate corals add to the finer particles of shell fragments and the skeletal remains of other animals and plants. As waves break across the reef there is a tendency for most of this material to be swept over and deposited behind it. Larger fragments of coral require much more energy to move than finer particles of well-ground sand. It follows that even during a storm, waves are likely to carry grains of sand much further into the reef backwaters than large boulders of dead coral. Even so, the space immediately behind the reef will infill most rapidly because it lies adjacent to the source of debris. The overall effect is the accumulation and sorting of sediments in the area enclosed by the reef, which may be a circular lagoon in the case of atolls and some patch reefs or a narrow lagoon between a fringing reef and an island.

Immediately behind the crest of a coral reef (usually defined by a hard pavement of cemented coral limestone which is known as the algal rim on Pacific reefs) is a zone of rubble. These barren drifts of coral skeletons are the cemeteries of storms. Rubble drifts are most common behind the exposed parts of reef crests and while most are covered by water at high tide, a few are large enough to remain constantly above the surface. These are the coral shingle cays; islands which can be spectacularly and almost miraculously born in the midst of a single raging storm.

Behind the rubble zone the debris becomes progressively finer, creating a gently shelving bed of sand. This region is called the reef flat and when viewed from the air is a dramatic turquoise colour. A fringing reef lying close to the mainland or to an island not only develops these distinctive 'back reef' zones, but also deposits debris on the nearby shoreline to form a coral-sand beach. Atoll reefs, on the other hand, encircle a body of water rather than an island, and sand gradually encroaches on and infills this central deep lagoon. The reef flat often forms the

Grand Cayman Island, 300km (186 miles) south of Cuba, lies adjacent to the deepest abyss in the Caribbean Sea. The Cayman Trench (commonly known as 'The Wall' due to its precipitous incline) drops to 7,535m (24,720ft) below sea-level. Using deep-sea submersibles, marine scientists have been able to study the different zones of life that occur at various depths. At its summit, the Cayman Wall is bathed in sunlight which enables a coral reef to thrive. Below 60m (200ft), however, much of the sunlight has been absorbed and reef-building hard corals give way to a community of sponges which filter the water for microscopic particles of plankton. Soft corals like the sea whip are also found here. Crustaceans, such as the Caribbean spiny lobster, forage for shellfish at depths approaching 180m (600ft). Beyond this level, sea lilies, resembling upside-down feathery starfish on stalks, begin to replace the sponges. As the wall plummets into inky blackness below 300m (1,000ft), bizarre deep-sea creatures, illuminated by the submersible's searchlights, appear against a lunar-like scene where everything is shrouded in a blanket of fine white sediment.

largest zone behind a coral reef and it is within this region that sandy coral cays may develop.

As waves break on the reef crest, their force is not totally absorbed. Miniature versions ripple out across the surface of the reef flat, and at high tide when the reef crest may be covered by several metres of water, conditions inside the reef may become quite choppy. In addition, there may be several passes or gaps in the reef through which larger waves can enter. All of these water movements develop into a characteristic pattern of sweeping currents which fan the sand particles into a particular part of the reef flat. Over time a submerged bank may form, rising in a shallow ridge above the sandy bottom. A series of high spring tides then nourish the sandbank, building it to a level which is overlapped less frequently. An island of coral sand emerges in tentative stages and to begin with the cay is restless, shifting its position on the reef flat as waves and currents tug and pull at the unstable sand.

The concentration of sediment in the reef flat and the formation of an embryoid cay may take thousands of years, but a tropical storm can deliver a single devastating blow, scattering the newly formed island beneath the surface again. If the island can endure its turbulent birth and unstable infancy, a whole range of processes begins to take place which help to consolidate it.

Unlikely as it seems, one of the major (albeit indirect) contributors to the island's stability are birds. Despite the fact that these coral cays, at such an early stage, are no more than a few square metres of shifting sand, sea-birds begin to roost on them. The surrounding waters of the reef flat and the deeper sea beyond the reef provide rich pickings of fish and squid, while the new piece of land acts as a useful resting platform. In time, large colonies of terns and other sea-birds begin to enrich the sterile coral sand with their droppings. The phosphate component of this so-called guano is carried by rain-water down into the heart of the cay where, by various chemical processes, it cements sand to form a stabilizing layer of buried cay sandstone. This band of hidden rock acts as an 'island anchor', resisting the tug of tidal currents.

The hard pan of sandstone traps subsequent rain-water above its impervious strata. This eventually develops into a subterranean basin of groundwater from which a solution of calcium carbonate leaks. Mineral-bearing water such as this permeates the surface levels of the developing cay and cements sand to produce a concrete-like band of beach rock.

Although the cay sandstone helps to maintain the centre of the cay in a fairly constant region of the reef flat by virtue of its

Mangroves are a group of tropical trees and shrubs that are adapted to life in the intertidal zone. A fringe of mangroves growing around the shoreline of a sand cay helps to consolidate the island by trapping additional quantities of sediment within its meshwork of roots. The mangroves also act as a buffer to waves and currents, reducing the impact of erosion. Mangroves can start their own island genesis process, leading to the formation of mangrove cays. These often begin forming in sheltered regions where suitable foundations such as dead coral platforms exist. The cay grows and matures as particles of fine sand and organic material accumulate beneath the mangrove trees. At the centre of the island this so-called 'mangrove mud' may be built up to levels that are only flooded by the highest tides, whereas the seaward margins of the cay are frequently overwashed.

solid properties, the shoreline is still continually reshaped by wave action and scouring currents. Waves and wind gradually begin exposing the newly formed beach rock and where erosion is most severe the beach rock is rapidly uncovered until it forms a shoreline barrier. This absorbs the impact of waves and protects the beach.

No coral cay can be regarded as completely stable. Beach rock and cay sandstone formation are continual processes. There are persistent, gnawing currents in one part of the island while in another the same water movements nourish the growth of new land. The coral island owes its existence to a dynamic struggle of natural forces: reef growth versus denudation, erosion versus deposition, movement versus stability and sea versus land.

However, the creation of a coral island represents far more than simply the by-product of these forces. Each new piece of land disgorged above the surface – whether a volcanic peak, a raised reef or a sandy coral cay – provides a unique opportunity for plant and animal colonization. The stage is set for a remarkable transformation as nature struggles to cloak each island in green, and populate it with wildlife.

During a violent cyclone a coral reef may suffer enormous damage. These pools were chiselled into the reef framework by storm-driven waves. In the decades since, vigorous coral growth has patched up the scars and, in time, the pools may be completely infilled by new reef-building corals.

■

39

BARE SAND TO THICK FOREST

CROSSING FRONTIERS

The spider hatchlings emerged in their hundreds from a protective cocoon of silk strung between two leaves. The adult female which laid her eggs in the fibrous nest a few weeks earlier had not stayed to guard her offspring when they hatched. The tiny spiders spilled from the nest, each a miniature version of an adult, prepared to face the hostile challenges of survival. Immediately, they began to scatter amongst the leaf blades and stems, the original writhing mass breaking into smaller radiating columns until the cocoon was left tattered and empty. Each individual went its own way, controlled by an instinct which dictated its behaviour. If all of the hatchlings had remained crowded near the nest they would have starved or become an easy target for predators. Their first response to being born was to disperse. Other driving forces helped to motivate this behaviour. Spiders, like all living species, try to colonize new habitats, establish new ranges and create new branches of evolution. All these things help to ensure long-term survival, but to cross frontiers and reach hidden lands or even remote islands in the midst of seas, an animal or plant must be capable of dispersal.

Soon the baby spiders had disappeared amongst the dense undergrowth. Some would spend their entire lives there, but many others were destined to embark upon a momentous journey. Clambering upwards they reached the seed heads of tall grasses which swayed slightly in a tentative breeze. Clinging to a stem, each spider raised its abdomen slightly, and from a group of small tubes called spinnerets, a long thread of gossamer emerged. The strand of silk remained attached to the spider and streamed out like a banner when the faintest air movement brushed past. With gossamer for a parachute, the spiders released their hold of the grass stems and floated away. Their

A tiny hatchling spider climbs amongst the swaying heads of grasses highlighted by the golden rays of a setting sun.

OPPOSITE
Coconut palms and hardy, salt-tolerant bushes thrive on a coral cay in the Caribbean Sea.

Beach rock often extends along part of a cay's shoreline, forming a low grey rampart between white coral-sand beach and blue shallow-water reef flat.

∎

destination was unknown; they had placed their future entirely at the mercy of the wind. It could carry these so-called 'ballooning' arachnids many hundreds of kilometres away from their birthplace. The vast majority would perish by being blown into the sea or onto inhospitable land. But wasting the lives of many is nature's way of increasing the chances of just a few individuals making landfall and colonizing new ground. Against all the odds, animals and plants have dispersed across formidable ocean barriers to populate islands throughout the world.

The presence of thriving communities of land plants and animals on remote islands has fascinated mankind for hundreds of years. As long ago as the fifth century, St Augustine came to

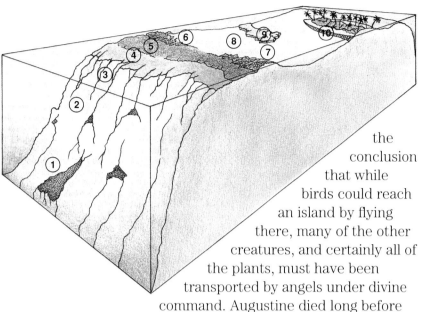

A cross-section through a generalized coral reef shows the distinctive pattern of zones that develop as a result of coral growth and erosion.

Key
1. Scree of eroded debris
2. Reef slope
3. Spur and groove
4. Reef crest
5. Zone of encrusting algae
6. Rubble drift
7. Coral rubble cay
8. Sandy reef flat
9. Patch reef
10. Coral sand cay

■

the conclusion that while birds could reach an island by flying there, many of the other creatures, and certainly all of the plants, must have been transported by angels under divine command. Augustine died long before the exploration of the great oceans began, and he would perhaps have been amazed to learn of the existence of islands such as Hawaii, lying in the middle of the Pacific, fully cloaked with green forests. It was not until the time of Darwin that serious biogeographical studies of island communities were started, and he discussed in *On the Origin of Species* some of his original ideas about how organisms colonized islands and were then able to survive in isolation. During his voyage aboard the *Beagle*, Charles Darwin actually witnessed the mass dispersal of juvenile spiders as they attempted to cross oceanic barriers. He observed this strange phenomenon while the vessel was more than 150km (93 miles) from the coast of South America. The entire rigging was draped with the silky threads of gossamer, each strand attached to a small spider.

Darwin was also aware that plants and animals could disperse across water by several other means, but in the years since the death of the great naturalist in 1882, our knowledge of dispersal and colonization has greatly increased.

Islands can obtain their fauna and flora by two means. A continental island is often formed when a land connection with the mainland becomes flooded. Animals and plants inhabiting the mainland would already have populated the future island before this link was broken. (This explains why all the continental coral islands lying near the Queensland coast of Australia have communities similar to the neighbouring mainland.) Some additional species may arrive by dispersal at a later stage.

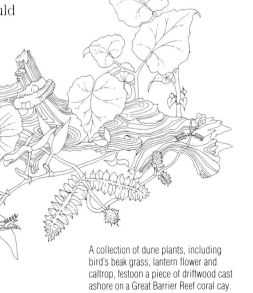

A collection of dune plants, including bird's beak grass, lantern flower and caltrop, festoon a piece of driftwood cast ashore on a Great Barrier Reef coral cay.

■

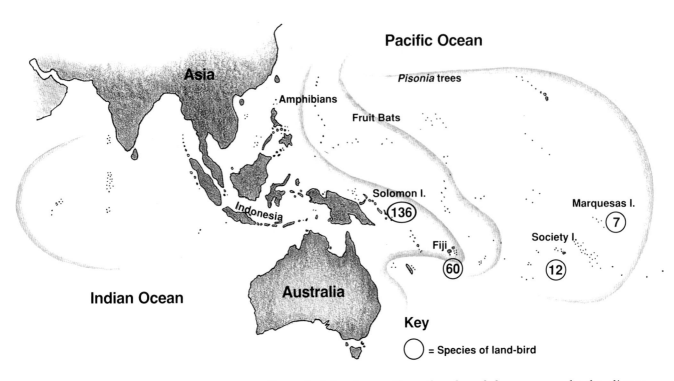

Pacific Ocean

Asia

Pisonia trees

Amphibians

Fruit Bats

Solomon I.
(136)

Marquesas I.
(7)

Society I.
(12)

Indonesia

Fiji
(60)

Indian Ocean

Australia

Key

◯ = Species of land-bird

The sticky seeds of the *Pisonia* tree have been dispersed by birds across a vast area of the tropical Indo-Pacific. The Pacific range of amphibians and fruit bats, however, is more restricted, and the diversity of land-birds decreases dramatically on the more remote islands.

■

Oceanic islands, on the other hand, have never had a direct connection with land and must receive all of their fauna and flora by dispersal across sea. This is the case with the majority of coral islands, including those with origins as volcanic islands, raised reefs and coral cays. To a large extent oceanic continental islands such as the Seychelles are also populated by species which travelled across sea.

The ease with which an island can be colonized depends on two main factors. The first is time, since the older an island is, the longer it will have been exposed to the opportunistic arrivals of potential colonists. Position is the second major factor. Islands lying near to continents have a greater chance of being colonized than mid-oceanic ones. This is reflected by the number of species found on different Pacific islands. A clear pattern emerges, with islands such as New Caledonia and the Solomon group possessing a greater number and wider variety of plants and animals than more far-flung islands such as Hawaii and the Marquesas. For example, sixty-eight species of land-bird inhabit New Caledonia while only seven are found in the Marquesas.

DISPERSAL

To succeed in reaching an isolated coral island an organism must be well adapted to the rigours of oceanic dispersal. An incredible variety of specializations have evolved which help certain plants and animals to disperse, and each of these is particularly suited to one of three types of carrier: the wind, the sea, or other mobile animals.

Wind dispersal is used by plants such as ferns and mosses,

Wave patterns and currents nourish the growth of a coral cay by depositing sand onto its shoreline.

OPPOSITE
A palm seedling bathed in sunlight filtering through the canopy of a tropical island forest.

■

44

which produce tiny, lightweight spores. The spores of some ferns may be less than 0.10mm (0.004in) in size and can easily be carried thousands of kilometres by the wind. The more advanced members of the Compositae family, including the dandelions and thistles, shed seeds with special flight devices such as feathery parachutes and tufts of fine hairs and are wafted in air currents.

Wind dispersal of animals is in many ways similar to that of plants. The likely candidates are all very small and released in huge numbers. Such creatures include mites, aphids and tiny flies. Countless millions of insects are constantly riding the streams of high-atmosphere winds where they are joined by the parachuting spiders on their strands of gossamer. A century after Charles Darwin was pondering the significance of the floating spiders that had descended into the rigging of the *Beagle*, a scientist called J. Linsley Gressitt was trapping wind-dispersed arthropods in nets trailed behind planes flying over islands in the Pacific. Gressitt found that the insects and spiders caught in the nets were of the same varieties as those living on the oceanic islands.

Crested terns race before a brisk ocean breeze. Strong fliers such as these are capable of colonizing remote oceanic islands.

Passive transport by wind does not account for the dispersal of all insects. Larger strong-flying types such as dragonflies, butterflies and locusts are capable of colonizing remote islands by a series of jumps from one archipelago to the next. Many of these movements are wind assisted, and certain species of butterfly are known to migrate to islands on the Great Barrier Reef, travelling the 60km (37 miles) from the mainland during periods of strong westerly breezes. Similarly, large dragonflies are frequently observed skimming the clear waters around coral cays on the Belize Barrier Reef, having flown across the 20km (12 mile) wide lagoon that separates the reef system from Central America.

The insect and spider faunas of a coral island are not, however, restricted to airborne species. How can the presence of large spiders and ground-dwelling centipedes, earwigs and cockroaches be accounted for? Violent offshore storms certainly have the power to dislodge and carry such creatures aloft (together with a horde of other insects and even birds), and sometimes they discharge their involuntary passengers onto nearby islands, but these hurricanes and gales also initiate other forms of dispersal. Trees and shrubs growing alongside a river may be torn from the ground and then swept downstream towards the sea, carrying with them a variety of animal refugees that had sought shelter amongst the vegetation as the winds struck. These fragile rafts of flotsam contain invertebrates such as snails, millipedes, centipedes, worms, ants, cockroaches and spiders, and occasionally a small backboned animal like a lizard

Restricted entirely to the Seychelle Islands in the Indian Ocean, the coco-de-mer is a giant species of palm which produces the world's largest and heaviest nuts. The trunk of the coco-de-mer may reach 30m (100ft) in height and each nut can weigh up to 20kg (50lbs). The nut resembles two huge coconuts welded together into a bi-lobed husk containing a solid mass of flesh around a central seed. The structure floats relatively short distances before sea-water kills it. This explains why the coco-de-mer is only found in the Seychelles and it also means that the palm must have evolved there. This dispels an ancient belief that the massive nuts washed up on the beaches of Arabia and India were the fruits of an aquatic tree; hence the name 'coco-de-mer'.

or amphibian may become trapped with the castaways. Once free of the swirling eddies at the river estuary, the rafts are carried away by ocean currents. The prospects of survival for many of their occupants are bleak.

Any amphibians on board will begin to dehydrate in the absence of moisturizing fresh-water, and unless the voyage is fairly rapid they will die. Frogs may take to the sea in a final desperate attempt to reach land, but the high salt content of the water will also spell death for them. Despite this seemingly hopeless situation, two species of frog have actually managed to colonize the islands of Fiji. Their successful dispersal is thought to have been made possible by the frogs' unusual breeding cycle. Both species lay eggs which hatch directly into miniature adults, missing out the tadpole stage which normally develops in fresh-water – an important adaptation if landfall happens to be made on a coral island with little or no surface-water. The eggs, being more resistant to salt water than the adults, could have survived the ocean crossing, secure within the curved frond of a palm, and hatched straight into small frogs on the beaches of Fiji.

Eggs are often better suited to dispersal than their adults, particularly for animals trapped on a raft of vegetation, since each embryo is neatly packaged with a food supply and contained within a fairly protective covering. An adult, on the

Plants and animals disperse across oceans using a variety of methods. Strong-flying animals such as terns, fruit bats and dragonflies (A) make short hops between island chains. Sea-birds and bats carry fleas and sticky or hooked plant seeds with them (B). Undigested seeds of fruits are dispersed inside their stomachs. Tiny insects are carried by the wind, along with hatchling spiders floating on strands of gossamer silk (C). Plants which produce feathery seeds or minute spores (D) are also wind-blown, whereas other plant seeds are packed in buoyant capsules (E) designed for floating in ocean currents. Driftwood and other pieces of flotsam transport small creatures such as lizards and ants (F) as well as burrowing termites and beetles or their eggs and larvae (G).

Nuts of the coconut palm make landfall on a Belize Barrier Reef coral cay. If high tide strands the coconuts far enough up the beach they may successfully complete their dispersal by germinating.

OPPOSITE
Anolid lizards have successfully colonized most of the islands in the Caribbean, rafting on floating vegetation from both South and Central America. This individual is basking on the trunk of a coconut palm.

other hand, is not even guaranteed food. This ultimately depends on the edibility of travelling companions or of the plants that make up the raft.

Considering all the trials of sea dispersal that these involuntary drifters must cope with in order to survive, it is not surprising to find that few, if any, terrestrial animals have reached coral islands by actually floating or swimming there. After all, a land creature that could swim several hundred kilometres across open ocean would probably have to be so perfectly adapted to an aquatic lifestyle that an entirely terrestrial existence on an island would be impossible. Some animals have made a compromise between the two. Turtles may haul themselves onto beaches to lay their eggs, but the adults spend the rest of their lives in the sea where they obtain food, mate and sleep. The Hawaiian monk seal is also essentially a marine species and will only drag itself out of the water to give birth, nourish its pups and bask in the sun on coral cays in Hawaii's Leeward Islands.

There is one coral island inhabitant, however, which is completely terrestrial in lifestyle, and is known to disperse by floating in ocean currents. On the remote raised atoll of Aldabra, lying over 400km (250 miles) north of Madagascar in the Indian Ocean, there are well over 100,000 giant tortoises. Some grow to 2m (6ft 8in) in length and weigh 200kg (440lb), but the giants of Aldabra are thought to have descended from much smaller varieties living on the African mainland. These normal sized tortoises were probably carried to Madagascar on rafts of floating vegetation. Being reptiles, tortoises possess a watertight skin that resists the desiccating effects of sea-water that amphibians find so difficult to tolerate. It is feasible that some young giant tortoises then made the onward journey north to Aldabra on drifts of flotsam, but it would not have been necessary. The adults are perfectly buoyant themselves and have been observed floating at sea for several days, feeding on seaweed and even holding their breath when swamped by large waves.

Adaptations for sea dispersal are, nevertheless, far more highly developed in members of the plant kingdom. The coastal fringes of most coral islands are dominated by plants which are washed up as floating seeds upon the beach. Several types of sea-borne seeds can be collected from the strand line in a matter of minutes. Perhaps the most conspicuous and well-known of these belongs to the coconut palm, which is widespread on tropical coasts throughout the world. This is partly a result of man's material interest in copra, the dried kernel of the coconut, which used to be a valuable commodity in the production of oils and animal feed. The speed at which the coconut radiated out

Giant tortoise from the Indian Ocean atoll of Aldabra.

The octopus bush has colonized coral islands throughout the world. This individual, growing on an island in the Maldives, has several coiled flower branches bearing small white flowers.

■

across the oceans from its native south-east Asia was increased by human efforts to establish plantations for the copra trade. Even so, coconut palms leaning out over the beach are able to drop their nuts within reach of waves and begin their own dispersal. Each nut is surrounded by a thick fibrous husk which encloses a hard-shelled seed, and the whole structure is perfectly buoyant. Coconuts can withstand up to four months floating at sea, allowing their dispersal over many hundreds of kilometres.

Other plants which disperse to coral islands as buoyant seeds include the sea cabbage and octopus bushes. Their fruits either contain numerous air cavities or are surrounded by a lightweight corky shell. Both these shrubs are characteristic of coral island shorelines. Sea-water actually inhibits their germination, but once the seeds are cast ashore, the first drenching of fresh rain-water reverses the process and signals that conditions are suitable for sprouting.

The *Pandanus* palm is another widespread species, producing large pineapple-shaped clusters of fruit which break up and float away on currents. Smaller buoyant fruits of the beach pea, beach morning glory and some grasses such as the bird's beak variety also disperse by sea.

An alternative to evolving a seed that is either light enough

50

to be carried away in a breeze or buoyant and waterproof enough to float at sea, is to develop some means of attaching it to a mobile animal. Birds and bats make excellent dispersal agents, and have, of course, colonized many coral islands themselves. Some species of wading birds incorporate stop-overs on oceanic islands as part of their annual migration, before returning to cooler climes to breed. Terns, frigatebirds, boobies, gulls and many other varieties of sea-bird rely on the oceans as their larders, and islands provide convenient predator-free nesting sites close to this essential resource. Land-birds, including pigeons, swifts, white-eyes and rails, as well as large bats like flying foxes, are often caught in strong offshore winds which carry them out to sea and into the path of islands. All of these flying creatures disperse across entire oceans (some have reached the most remote archipelagoes), island-hopping and establishing new colonies at each suitable landfall, but they are probably unaware of the seeds and animals they carry with them.

A trio of crested terns rest on a pile of coral rubble after a fishing sortie. The bird on the left has a speckled forehead which distinguishes it from the two mature breeding adults next to it.

■

Found on islands throughout the Indian and Pacific Oceans, the mournful gecko is a particularly accomplished colonizer. It lays sticky, salt-resistant eggs under the bark of trees which may be carried to islands as floating pieces of driftwood. Adults are also known to make landfall by rafting ashore on driftwood. Only one mournful gecko needs to colonize an island in order to establish a flourishing population, since females are able to lay fertile eggs without any assistance from a male. This is known as parthenogenesis, and on many islands the mournful gecko community consists entirely of females.

Some seeds, such as those of the caltrop, bear spikes that snag on the feet of ground-nesting sea-birds. Even plants which have not gone to the trouble of evolving clever means of seed attachment may be dispersed in mud caked around a bird's foot. The ripe fruits of the *Pisonia* tree are sticky and attach themselves to any birds brushing past. So effective is this glue-like secretion that black noddies, which nest in *Pisonia* trees, sometimes become totally smeared in the substance and face starvation because they are unable to fly and catch food. Another example of a plant using sticky fruits as a tactic for dispersal is the tar-vine which grows along the surface amongst ground-nesting birds.

Other plants produce edible fruits containing small seeds which can be dispersed within the digestive systems of fruit-eating bats and birds. The seeds of figs, mulberries and nightshade can withstand the enzymatic rigours of digestion and are eventually voided in the droppings. In addition to plants, birds and bats also transport ectoparasites such as ticks, lice and fleas.

By this incredible array of dispersal techniques, plants and animals are continually arriving on coral islands. Whether a ballooning spider, a cockroach washed up on a piece of driftwood, a bird blown from the mainland or a coconut swept onto a beach, these organisms have challenged vast oceans and succeeded in reaching new land. But making landfall on a coral island is only the start of a series of problems. The new arrivals must survive and reproduce to ensure that the colonizing efforts they have made so far have not been in vain.

To appreciate fully their trials and failures and to

understand how they eventually manage to succeed, it is interesting to speculate and follow the development of a single hypothetical island.

THE FIRST COLONIZERS

When a coral cay first emerges as a low bank of sand it is completely devoid of terrestrial life. It is nothing more than a sterile featureless platform. The fierce tropical sun scorches its entire surface, for there are no trees to cast any shade. An incessant ocean breeze sprays the island with salty mists and fans sand into shifting, unstable ripples, which resemble a miniature desert landscape. Nutrients are scarce and rain-water, when it falls, either evaporates or is turned salty as it drains away through the coral sand. These are the harsh realities facing the potential colonist. What kind of terrestrial plant or animal could possibly endure such conditions?

By chance, a few feathery seeds of a flowering plant blow onto the tiny island, and the storm that has driven them half-way across an ocean delivers a deluge of fresh rain-water before it scuds away. The seeds germinate and small green shoots unwind from capsules that have been rapidly buried in the moving sand. For a brief moment it seems that life is underway. By the following day however, each seedling is dead, choked by sand and withered by salt and sun. This particular species was not destined to pioneer the colonization process. Many other types of plants and animals will arrive before conditions on the island can sustain them, and one by one they too will perish.

Unlikely as it seems, the sea provides the first opportunity for terrestrial life to flourish on the juvenile sandy coral island. Each high tide strands an assortment of flotsam, and in amongst the cuttlefish bones, pieces of broken sponges and algae, are the dead remains of fish, crabs and jellyfish. A seafood banquet is laid out and a small colony of wind-borne scavenging beetles make it their home. In time, small spiders descend on the island and are able to survive by hunting the beetles. The first community is established, and gradually it diversifies as gnats, earwigs, mites and centipedes arrive.

Animals often successfully colonize islands before plants. These early scavenger–predator communities effectively by-pass the need for plants and herbivores because they can rely totally on the high productivity of the sea to provide for all their needs. Burrowing under decaying piles of stranded algae and seagrass, they find conditions that are cool and damp, ideal for laying eggs. When new generations of scavengers emerge there is plenty of food for them to eat, but their numbers are kept in balance by the predators.

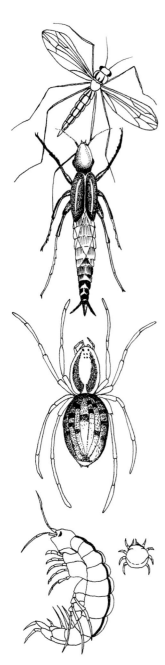

This community of animals, including (*from top to bottom*) a gnat, beetle, spider, mite and sand-hopper (or amphipod) is resident amongst the strand line of a coral cay on the Belize Barrier Reef.

The sea plays another indirect but vital role in the colonization process. Ground-nesting sea-birds such as black-naped terns, crested terns and masked gannets begin to use the bare island platforms for roosting and nesting, and some of the richness of the sea is effectively transferred to the island in the form of their droppings. This has two effects. Firstly, it provides another source of food for scavenging invertebrates and the wind-blown spores of decomposers such as bacteria and fungi, and secondly, it fertilizes the island with a rich source of nutrients including nitrates and phosphates. The transfer is intensified during the breeding season when adults are feeding their chicks. During this period some nestlings will die and become another component of the nutrient pathway that links the rich sea with the once sterile island.

Despite this gradual fertilization, conditions are still far from hospitable for most types of vegetation, and the first plants that can endure the blowing sand and salt spray are well-adapted pioneers. These species often have thick, waxy stems and leaves which help them to withstand salt and tolerate drought. Sometimes their leaves are slightly curled to further reduce water loss. They grow low to the ground, offering little resistance to the wind. To cope with shifting sand, pioneer plants spread rapidly, creating a mesh of intertwined creeping stems so that if one part is buried or uprooted another section can continue to

The strand line provides food and a home for small scavenging insects and also contains the seeds of floating sea-borne plants, a few of which have already sprouted wiry shoots.

■

This field illustration portrays four species of pioneer plants that are well adapted to the hostile shoreline conditions on South Water Cay (Belize Barrier Reef). A small beetle, 4mm (0.16in) in length, is one of the only animals that inhabit this region.

nourish it. Other varieties germinate and then put all of their energy into producing seeds as soon as possible. The adult plants may then wither and die, but the species maintains a precarious foothold on the island since the scattered seeds will sprout after the next period of rainfall and repeat the process.

Using these tactics, pioneer plants are able to colonize coral cays. Common species include bird's beak grass, beach pea, beach morning glory and sea purslane. These plants are not, however, totally immune to some of the more extreme conditions which face a young coral island. Frequently their efforts to become established are hampered by storm-driven waves, or trampling from crowded colonies of sea-birds. The digging habits of nesting sea turtles, which excavate large pits in which to lay their eggs, can also be very destructive to plant life. Indeed, many coral islands which reach the stage of being carpeted with pioneer vegetation are degraded so severely that plant colonization must start all over again.

Over many years, and even decades, the pioneer plants will eventually become thoroughly established, and in amongst the sparse covering of vines and grasses a few herbivorous insects may find a suitable source of food to reward their chance landfall.

CHANGING HABITATS

Pioneer vegetation is an essential stage of colonization because it modifies conditions on the coral island in two fundamental ways. Firstly, the networks of vines and grasses embrace and stabilize the sand surface. Secondly, wind-blown grains are trapped by leaves and stems and begin to accumulate as small dunes around the edge of the island. The pioneers have made it possible for other less robust plants to colonize. Species which have little tolerance for salt can now begin to grow on the protected leeside of sand dunes, and the floating seeds of shoreline plants can germinate more easily in the firmer substrate.

When one group of plants creates conditions that enable another to colonize, the process is known as succession. Certain plants will only be able to colonize once their specific soil and climate requirements can be satisfied, and this in turn depends on how advanced succession is. At this early stage, the coral island has two zones of succession: a fringing coastal area of salt and drought-resistant pioneer plants, and a central sheltered region which retains more rain-water and supports less hardy species.

Dune formation continues, and not only builds the island higher but increases its overall area as well. This attracts more species of birds, some with the intention of breeding and others

A Caribbean pioneer grass forms a spreading mesh across the beach sands of a coral cay.

which will only frequent the island as a roosting site. More varieties of terns and gannets arrive, along with red-tailed tropic-birds and lesser frigatebirds. Many will carry the hooked or sticky seeds of plants that grow on islands they have recently visited, and these may drop to the ground and germinate.

Floating seeds of the octopus bush, stranded on the seaward slope of the sand dunes by a receding tide, begin to flourish. Eventually this species, together with the sea cabbage bush, *Pandanus* palm, *Casuarina* tree and *Suriana* shrub will form an entire ring of dense scrub around an Indo-Pacific island. On Belize Barrier Reef cays, another addition to the littoral fringe is the red-barked gombo limbo tree.

Tall *Pandanus* palms stabilize themselves against strong winds with clusters of small prop roots which emerge from the base of their trunks. These have the added benefit of allowing the palms to lean slightly over the beach so that when their ripe floating fruits drop, they are carried away on the tide. The coconut palm, another shoreline species, often grows out across the beach at an even more precarious angle due to its shallow root system and lack of any structural support. A severe storm can undermine its grip on the sands so completely that the palm is sent toppling into the sea.

A crested tern preens in the final moments before sunset. These terns breed in dense island colonies throughout the Indian Ocean, around south-east Asia and Australia and in the central and western Pacific. Pairs make a depression in sand or shingle in which a single egg is laid.

■

Shrubs and grasses have trapped sand to form dunes two or three metres (about six or ten feet) in height on Heron Island, a mature coral cay on the Great Barrier Reef.

■

Certain species of butterfly whose caterpillars feed on the thick leaves of the octopus bush or sea cabbage bush can now become resident members of the island fauna. The adults feed on nectar from the shrubs' small clusters of flowers and, in doing so, provide a pollination service. Small moths and aphids also join the growing insect community, together with predatory bugs and beetles and scavenging ants.

The shrub ring represents the next major step in plant succession for it effectively shields the island's interior from wind and salt spray. This allows the herbs that first began to grow tentatively in the lee of the dunes to flourish. Delicate orange blooms of the lantern flower and sea trumpet, together with yellow caltrop and white convolvulus, unfurl for the attention of shiny black bees. New leaves and stems replace old and dying ones which fall to the ground and begin to decay. The resulting humus, vitalized by the nutrients in sea-bird guano, creates a rich fertilizer on which a greater abundance and variety of plants can thrive. The luxuriant growth shades the ground and prevents the moist leaf-litter from drying out.

Deep within the island a buried lens of rain-water has been accumulating, becoming less brackish as the island gains height above the sea. With shelter, fertilizer and a source of water that can be tapped by large root systems, the island's interior is ready for trees. Flocks of fruit-eating birds, such as white-eyes, blown out to sea and too weak to fly back to the mainland, void the seeds of fig and mulberry trees in their droppings. Each seed lands on the ground with an additional supply of fertilizer, and in time an open parkland with scattered trees and bushes develops. Eventually this mixed wood dominates the central region of the island, leaving only isolated clearings of grasses and herbs.

Various land-birds can now colonize the island. Some species that arrive will be more successful at colonizing than others. For example, a lone male falcon stranded on an oceanic island is doomed to a short-term colonization. A pair of falcons or even a single pregnant female would stand a greater chance of establishing a viable population. This explains why social flocking birds like white-eyes and starlings make good colonists: a group of birds is likely to contain at least one breeding pair.

Another useful characteristic to possess is a degree of flexibility. A bird that occupies a very specific habitat on the mainland will not appreciate being blown out to sea and deposited on a coral cay. Scientists at the research station on Heron Island in the Capricorn Group of the Great Barrier Reef, frequently record the arrival of such unfortunate birds. A black swan makes a dramatic sight as it glides gracefully across the turquoise waters of the reef flat, but there are no freshwater

The Capricorn silvereye, a member of the white-eye family, is well established on the coral islands at the southern end of the Great Barrier Reef. This small, flocking bird was probably responsible for establishing the islands' first sandpaper fig trees by carrying the seeds in its stomach from the Australian mainland.

OPPOSITE
A pair of *Pandanus* palms lean against prevailing winds, supported by the buttressed pillars of their roots. This plant is widespread in tropical Asia and can be found on coral islands between East Africa and Polynesia.

■

Kingfishers have successfully colonized many coral islands around the world. The sacred kingfisher, shown here, inhabits islands in the south-west Pacific including the Solomons and New Caledonia.

■

plants for it to feed on. Unless the swan can summon the energy to fly back to its resident lake on the mainland it faces certain death. A noisy pitta, swept from its home in the coastal rainforests of Queensland, may fare better. Although there is no rainforest on a coral cay like Heron Island, the pitta's habit of turning over leaf-litter to reveal its prey can be just as rewarding in the island's woodland. The pitta might not be a permanent colonist, but at least it will find enough food to build its strength for a homeward journey. By other means of feeding flexibility the warblers, shrikes, cuckoos and bee-eaters that are blown to Heron Island convalesce for a few days and then fly back to Australia.

Several other types of bird are able to stay permanently, and guarantee their success as colonists by breeding. Kingfishers chisel out nesting holes in the trunks of trees while doves gather small twigs for nests in bushes. Rails prefer to raise their young in the dense ground cover of grassy woodland clearings.

Maturing fruit trees begin to provide a source of food for many small birds and flying foxes. On coral cays in the Caribbean, tiny hummingbirds become resident breeding species, feeding from flowering shrubs and trees including the coconut palm. Anolid lizards, also widespread in this region, bask on tree trunks and exploit the insect fauna which is now abundant and diverse. The voracious appetite of larger herbivorous insects such as locusts can now be sustained, so long as predators such as kingfishers and large hunting spiders control their populations.

At any stage in the island's development, a link in the food chain between two species may break down. For example, a plant species can be eaten into extinction by a herbivore that has no predator to maintain its numbers. Of course, once the plant has vanished, the herbivore will rapidly become extinct as well, unless it can find a suitable alternative food source. There is no guarantee that a carnivore, specialized to eat this herbivore, will ever colonize the island. In these circumstances an intriguing cycle commences whereby the eradicated plant manages to recolonize only to be forced into extinction again if the herbivore also makes landfall.

Periodic colonization and extinction such as this is common in the story of life on a coral cay. At any one moment in the island's existence, its floral and faunal composition may be widely different to that of a few weeks earlier. Storms and droughts have a similar impact. In 1968, One Tree Island on the Great Barrier Reef suffered a drought that forced half its insect and spider population into extinction. The same species, living on the mainland, would have survived by seeking shelter and alternative places in which to live, feed and breed. Coral cays, however, are

Hundreds of black noddies voluntarily gather on the ground at midday in order to sunbathe. Tilting their heads to one side, fanning their tails and spreading one wing across their backs, they bask in the intense heat of a tropical sun. As bizarre as this behaviour may seem it is likely that it performs a vital role in ridding the noddies of annoying parasites such as fleas and bird ticks.

too small and isolated to provide such comforts from bad weather. The only solution is the harsh reality of recolonization when conditions are more favourable.

The bruised belly of a storm scuffles the flank of a coral reef. Severe hurricanes or cyclones can whip the sea into a foaming fury, causing extensive damage to corals and threatening the populations of island life that have limited places in which to shelter.

∎

THE CLIMAX FORESTS

Once the open woodland is well established, tree-nesting sea-birds may establish breeding colonies. Reef herons build untidy nests of twigs within the branches of sandpaper fig trees and *Pandanus* palms. Black noddies crowd the limbs of octopus bushes in such numbers that their guano turns the ground beneath them white. The nutrients within the droppings benefit the plant life, but the noddies play another important role in the island's development. Many bring the sticky seeds of *Pisonia* trees smeared to their feathers, and in the sheltered, fertile interior of the cay these are able to germinate. At first, just one or two *Pisonia* trees emerge, forming isolated clumps amongst the woodland. Then, gradually, the thickets of *Pisonia* coalesce to form a small forest at the very heart of the island, where conditions are most ideal.

The emergence of the forest signals a transition to the final stage, or climax, of plant succession. In the Indo-Pacific the natural climax vegetation is the *Pisonia* tree, while on Caribbean coral cays this role belongs to the orange-flowered siricote tree. Both the *Pisonia* and siricote displace the woodland to form a

The seedling of a *Pisonia* tree germinates in the sheltered heart of a forest on a Pacific coral cay.

■

dense central forest. The coral cay is now at its most mature. No other level of plant life or new habitat succeeds the forest.

As the forest matures and forms a closed canopy, fallen leaves build up into a thick leaf-litter teeming with cockroaches, centipedes and springtails. Black noddies now nest within the forest, enriching the leaf-litter with their huge amounts of guano. The burrowing activities of insects, land crabs and even tunnel-nesting birds such as shearwaters, help to transfer this organic material into the soil. The resulting humus retains moisture and provides a rich source of nutrients, enabling the climax forest to flourish.

A mature coral cay, having reached its climax stage of plant succession, reflects its earlier development in a series of concentric rings or zones surrounding the central forest. Impinging on the borders of the forest is a remnant of the open parkland, around which the shrub ring still crowns the crest of dunes before giving way to pioneer plants on the beach.

From the wave-swept sands that originally emerge above the sea, a coral cay can evolve into a complex array of different habitats, driven by the environmental modelling of succession and nourished by the constant landfall of dispersing animals and plants.

CLAIMING THE HIGH LAND

The colonization of a high volcanic coral island is, in many ways, similar to that of a low sandy one. Plants and animals must still disperse across the sea to reach a terrestrial speck, and after making landfall they must possess suitable adaptations and lifestyles in order to survive and breed.

However, the hardened flows of lava that form the surface of a young volcanic island present a different challenge to pioneer plants than the wind-blown sands of a coral cay. The once molten basalt has no loose grains of soil in which roots can anchor themselves. Airborne seeds are swept across the dark crusty deserts of lava and perish along with the spiders and insects which are carried to the island by wind. Most of their remains are blown out to sea, but occasionally pieces of debris are trapped in sheltered crevices and chinks in the lava flow. Moisture-laden air rising up the steep flanks of the island volcano, condenses and then falls as rain. Small rivulets of fresh-water snake down the slopes and begin to etch slight depressions in the hard rock, eroding tiny flakes of minerals which gather in the cracks already containing the dead insects and seeds. This mixture of fragments forms a thin layer of the most basic soil, but it is just sufficient to allow the spores of a moss to germinate. The moss spreads into a low-lying pad which soaks up rain-water like a sponge, retaining

The production of leaf-litter is an essential component in the life-support system on a coral cay since it recycles valuable nutrients into the soil.

OPPOSITE
Leaves of an octopus bush frame a pair of black noddies which have begun building their nest.

■

Low-lying bushes and a tall stand of
coconut palms fringe the northern
shoreline of Rarotonga; a high island in
the central South Pacific.

■

On 27 August 1883, the tiny volcanic island of Krakatoa, lying in the middle of the Sunda Strait between Java and Sumatra, exploded with devastating force. Ash that was fired into the atmosphere during the eruption fell back to earth over 6,000km (3,730 miles) away and two-thirds of the original island was eradicated. All plant and animal life vanished. Fourteen years later, however, more than one hundred species of insects, spiders and birds, together with sixty varieties of plants, had recolonized the remaining fragments of Krakatoa. In the late 1920s, a new active volcanic island emerged from the seas where Krakatoa's mountainous crater had once stood. The island, named Anak Krakatoa ('Son of Krakatoa'), is steadily growing, providing another source of unclaimed land for plants and animals to colonize.

moisture that had previously evaporated in the heat. Now ferns tentatively unfurl their fronds, emerging above the moss-filled crevices which supply them with water and nutrients. With shelter provided by the plant life, small scavenging insects colonize these tiny green pockets and feed on the remains of dispersal casualties. Like the scavenger–predator communities that develop beneath the strand line of a coral cay, hunters such as spiders and beetles can now become established.

These are the first signs of life that appear on the slopes of a volcanic island. Over several more decades of persistent weathering by rain and wind, the solid surface of the lava will gradually yield increasing amounts of soil and valuable trace

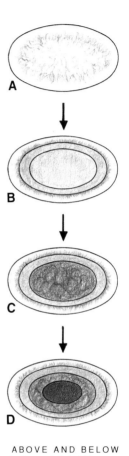

ABOVE AND BELOW
The development of plant life on a coral cay has four main stages. An island of bare sand is colonized by low-lying pioneer grasses and vines (A). Dunes, which form around the edge of the island, are crowned by a ring of shrubs (B) which shelter the interior and provide suitable conditions for the growth of a woodland (C). Eventually, the woodland begins to be displaced by a central forest (D). The whole process of plant succession may take several thousand years to complete. A cross-section (below) through a mature cay clearly shows each stage.

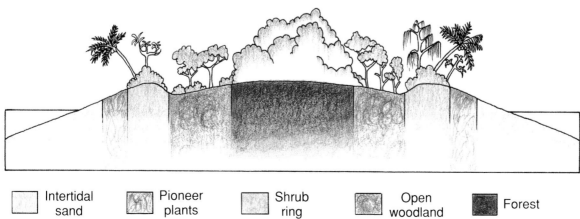

Intertidal sand	Pioneer plants	Shrub ring	Open woodland	Forest

OPPOSITE
The central rainforest of a high island contains a diverse collection of trees, shrubs and vines, but many of these may have been introduced by man.

■

A *Casuarina* tree clings precariously to a huge boulder of basalt, gradually weakening joints in the rock with its probing root system. *Casuarina* trees have two features which enable them to survive in poor soils, or even on the weathered surface of a boulder. Firstly, they possess root nodules that contain bacteria capable of harnessing atmospheric nitrogen, and secondly, they have tiny scale-like leaves which reduce excess evaporation of water from their tissues.

■

minerals in which plants can gain a foothold. The tireless pounding of the sea has the same effect around the island's steep shoreline, but here the eroded particles begin to form a beach of black sand. As a fringing coral reef starts to grow on the submerged shoulders of the island it donates white fragments of eroded coral to the beach. Little by little the island succumbs to the gnawing grip of the sea and the scouring lash of the weather. The crater that once spewed fire and molten rock begins to crack and crumble. Fallen screes of rock are embraced in strangleholds of creeping vines. The roots of hardy bushes and trees seek weaknesses in the ancient lava flows, twisting and writhing along narrow cracks and cleaving boulders in two. Uncoordinated trickles of rain-water become purposeful streams which feed gushing rivers. The crater collapses; huge rock slides gouge its flanks, dragging down towering walls of basalt with them. Then a haze of green begins gradually to obscure the gashes of raw rock as forests lay claim to the island's interior.

The shoreline of a high coral island is colonized by the same plants and animals that initiate succession on a low coral cay. Dunes built from the binding action of pioneer plants support a ring of shrubs and palms which, in turn, give rise to sheltered regions colonized by low herbs and then woodland and so on. However, on a high island, plant succession does not end with a forest of *Pisonia* or siricote trees. These species may well become established on the narrow coastal plain, but they are poorly adapted for colonizing the mountain slopes that rear up from the interior. Instead, the high land is claimed by a separate succession of plant types, pioneered by mosses and ferns and eventually reaching its climax with a plant type that is particularly suited to each altitude zone. Thus, the lower foothills become cloaked in thick tropical rainforest, the higher exposed moorlands with heathers and ferns and the rocky summits can support no more than the simple pioneer mosses and lichens. In addition to these broad vegetation zones, streams, cliff faces, rock screes and a range of other smaller niches offer different opportunities to suitable colonizers.

Hundreds or thousands of years may pass between the fiery birth of a volcanic island and the appearance of a rainforest on its weathered flanks. After several million years, the once towering peak will be eroded to little more than a small rounded hill. If this was an island lying in a cool temperate sea, it would subsequently vanish without trace below the waves. However, when a high island sinks below a tropical sea it continues to support the coral reef that first began growing in its coastal waters. The reef then becomes an atoll dotted with low sandy coral islands.

THE LIVING REEF

A CORAL REEF EXPERIENCE

The stingrays, lying in the shallows of the reef flat, had sensed the subtle swing of currents that heralded an ebbing tide and were preparing to move to the safe depths of the lagoon. The largest individual measured over two metres from the tip of its whip-like tail to its pointed snout. This was only evident, however, when the ray gently shook the covering of sand from its back and, on undulating wings, rose from the sea-bed and began to glide away across the reef flat like the shadow of a passing cloud. The other stingrays followed, accompanied by several blue-spotted lagoon rays and a shoal of sand coloured shovel-nose rays. Their departure to deeper water was hidden by swirling sand, agitated by the rays' elongated pectoral fins rippling into action.

A shoal of tiny black and white striped humbug damselfish darted into the sandy haze, flicking back and forth in pursuit of exposed food morsels. Their activity attracted a group of larger silver-bodied emperors and a single Picasso triggerfish with blue and yellow lips. Soon the water was filled by a swirling mass of fish, rushing to snatch the food stirred up by the rays' departure. A goatfish ploughed head first through the sandy bottom, feeling for worms and crustaceans with a pair of long sensory barbels wriggling from its chin. The triggerfish followed in its wake, pausing occasionally to pick at a fragment missed by the goatfish. A pair of sandy coloured gobies cautiously approached in a series of short swimming hops, pausing to rest on the bottom with splayed pectoral fins at each stop.

Suddenly a larger fish streaked in amongst them and the feeding foray ended as quickly as it had started. The damselfish retracted into a tight shoal and darted for the sanctuary of a small patch of branching coral lying nearby. The gobies vanished into a nearby burrow and the other fish took flight. Meanwhile,

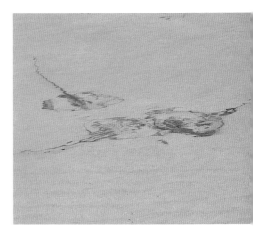

Most species of stingray are bottom-dwellers and camouflage themselves by lying partly buried on a sandy sea floor. These three individuals are resting in the shallow waters of a reef flat on the Great Barrier Reef. If threatened, they are capable of defending themselves by lashing out with three sharp barbs located on top of their tails.

OPPOSITE
A shoal of black-footed clownfish find sanctuary from predators within the stinging tentacles of a giant sea anemone. This species, together with Clark's clownfish, is common in the Maldives. They avoid competition for space by occupying different varieties of anemone; the black-footed clownfish is usually associated with long-tentacled forms, while Clark's clownfish inhabits those with much shorter tentacles.

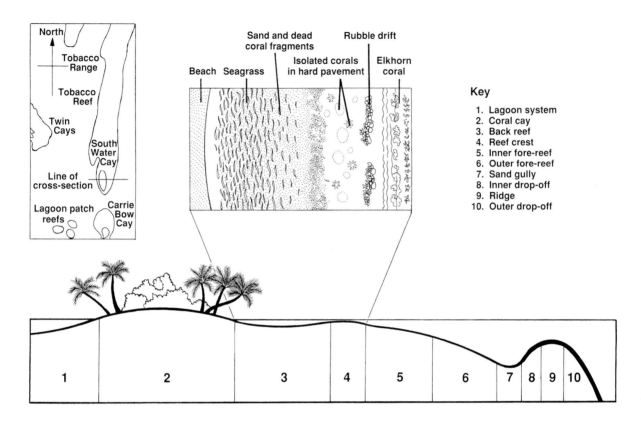

Key

1. Lagoon system
2. Coral cay
3. Back reef
4. Reef crest
5. Inner fore-reef
6. Outer fore-reef
7. Sand gully
8. Inner drop-off
9. Ridge
10. Outer drop-off

A generalized zonation of the Belize Barrier Reef is illustrated by this cross-section based on the South Water Cay region. A field sketch shows the back reef and reef crest in more detail. The inner fore-reef is the most biologically diverse zone. Seaward of the ridge, which lies between 15 and 30m (49 and 98ft) deep, is the outer drop-off which plummets for several hundred metres to the ocean floor.

the intruder, a black-tip reef shark, circled for a second charge unaware that its prey had already fled to shelter. With a taut flick of its tail, the shark returned to shallow cruising.

The sandy reef flat with its small isolated patches of dead and living coral is by no means the richest or most exotic habitat on a coral reef, and yet it contains a wealth of different species. Further out, towards the reef crest and beyond to the plummeting wall of the reef slope, there is a far greater diversity and abundance of fish and other reef-dwelling creatures. Whether snorkelling in the calm shallows of the reef flat, or scuba diving in front of the reef slope, the human visitor cannot fail to marvel at the prolific life.

A group of privileged divers enters a world muted by a wash of blue; a world totally silent apart from the rhythmic rush of air and ripple of bubbles from their breathing. Descending slowly, they gradually rotate to absorb the spectacular panorama of the reef spreading out below. The structure is inconceivably massive and yet intricately sculptured with a whole array of corals and sponges. Fish are everywhere. Several huge Maori wrasse, 1.5m (5ft) in length, wallow in the clear waters, rolling an inquisitive eye at the human intruders. Blue and white streaked cleaner wrasse dart into the mouths of their giant cousins, performing a dental valet by removing trapped pieces of food and tiny parasites, and then exiting through the pulsing gill covers. A

forest of tall yellow and purple staghorn coral sweeps down from the reef crest, and dancing between the stony antlers is a shoal of a hundred parrotfish. Butterfly fish, donning the colours of a rainbow, swoop and flit through the outreaching fingers of coral. Tiny jewel-speckled gobies with wide staring eyes rest on the narrow brittle branches. A scarlet-coloured shrimp tentatively emerges from cover, feeling its way with long sweeping antennae and pausing as a slender filefish with striking green and orange markings brushes past.

Corals grow in an incredible variety of shapes and sizes to produce a complex reef structure that offers a myriad of living opportunities for other creatures. This scene depicts a reef crest at North Male Atoll in the Maldives.

∎

Leaf corals forming a delicate maze of thin yellow-green walls become interspersed with the red branching lattice-works of gorgonian sea fans as the divers continue their descent. Brain corals grow in huge amorphous knolls while fern-like hydroids conceal their painful sting with an innocent display of alluring white plumes. Orange and yellow feather stars clutch at floating plankton, their outspread arms swaying in the reef currents. The same surging movements pulse giant anemones into rippling undulations, their fleshy folds of tentacles swirling to reveal a shoal of clownfish which are immune to the stinging cells of their home. Under the overhangs of jutting platform corals, writhing masses of nocturnal squirrelfish and cardinal fish await twilight before emerging.

At 30m (98ft) below the surface the divers pause and then roll on their sides to gaze back at the reef slope they have just

descended. The near-vertical wall of coral towers above them, reaching towards a sky made from the undersides of silver blue waves. Near its summit an enormous shoal of small fish rides the swell and tumbles below the waves, effortlessly moving as a single unit like a flock of birds embracing an ocean breeze. Sunlight filtering through the surface is split into flickering rays that reflect shards of silver from the fishes' bodies. The divers hang in watery space; below them the reef foundations plummet a further thousand metres, but all they can distinguish is the blurred outline of the wall before it is obscured by the impenetrable ink blue of deep water. As more light is absorbed by the increasing depth of water, the sun-dependent reef corals become less numerous and are replaced by sponges, growing in long ropy strands or forming huge barrel-shaped colonies. A large grouper with wide gulping mouth cruises past and then vanishes into the shadowy forest of sponges.

As the divers begin their ascent, a hawksbill turtle glides into view, propelled by an elegant sweeping synchrony of all four flippers. Sunlight ripples across the reptile's domed shell as it stalls into a graceful drift towards the surface. The creature pauses, its head above the water to take a deep breath which will sustain it for two hours, and then slowly sinking it rotates and rolls away on velvet flipper strokes.

The divers surface. The sky is an unbroken tower of cobalt blue and the tropical sun, tempered by a slight ocean breeze, is comfortably warm. Beauty aside, the world of the coral reef they have just experienced is unsurpassed by any other region of the sea in terms of its diversity and abundance of life. The Great Barrier Reef alone is home to over four hundred varieties of coral, some 1,500 species of fish and literally tens of thousands of different sponges, worms, clams, crabs, snails, slugs, sea urchins, starfish and other invertebrates, not to mention a diverse collection of marine algae.

It is ample satisfaction to witness the visual spectacle of a coral reef, but to appreciate some of the processes that enable it to function adds a fascinating new dimension. Coral reefs are perhaps the most complex ecosystems on earth and our understanding of how they work is still in its infancy, but the accumulation of this knowledge is essential. Only after a reef has been studied in detail can we hope to be aware of its requirements for survival and its susceptibility to man's activities, and only then can we act sensibly to safeguard it for the future.

A pair of yellow vase-shaped sponges protrude from a coral boulder on a Caribbean reef.

OPPOSITE

At low tide, the Pacific red reef hermit crab often clambers over exposed coral boulders in the reef flat, searching for animal and plant debris on which to feed. It also hunts for live molluscs such as trochus snails which are prised from their shells by the crab's tenacious pincers.

When two growing coral colonies encounter each other's margins, a slow but deadly battle may ensue. Some corals launch their attack by extending long sweeper tentacles armed with batteries of potent stinging cells into their opponents. Others, such as the mushroom coral, secrete a stinging mucus to maintain their living space. Another coral resists being overgrown simply by disgorging a bundle of enzyme-laden filaments from its gut, which can digest the living tissues of its rival within hours.

THE CROWDED COMMUNITY

One of the most striking features of a coral reef is the immense concentration of different creatures that live on, around and

OPPOSITE
Five varieties of triggerfish commonly
encountered on the reefs of the Maldives
include (*from top to bottom*) red-toothed
triggerfish, Picasso triggerfish, titan
triggerfish, orange-lined triggerfish and
clown triggerfish. Each possesses a
dorsal spine which when erected can
securely lock the fish into a narrow
crevice as a means of protection from
predators. Experienced fishermen can
'trigger' the lowering of the raised spine
by carefully pressing the two smaller
ones behind it.

■

**The remora is a long,
slender fish which is
frequently observed
clinging to the
undersides of large
sharks and manta rays,
achieving an effortless
means of transportation.
It uses a sucking disc,
located on the top of its
head, to securely and
harmlessly fasten itself.
Fishermen in the Indo-
Pacific use remoras to
catch turtles. Once a
turtle is sighted, a
captive sucker fish with
a line tied around its tail
is thrown into the sea,
and invariably swims
towards the marine
reptile and attaches
itself. The line is then
pulled taut (preventing
the remora from
releasing its suction
grip) and both fish and
turtle can be hauled in.**

within its complex three-dimensional frame. Immediately
noticeable are the fish and, of course, the corals themselves, but
many other animals including a seemingly infinite variety of
invertebrates are largely hidden amongst the cracks and crevices
of the reef. Only upon close inspection are the secret lives of tiny
crabs, worms and sea slugs revealed. In this crowded community
every vacant living-space is strongly contested, and some species
have gone to extraordinary lengths to find a home.

Clownfish and occasionally a few juvenile domino
damselfish, for example, find shelter amongst the stinging
tentacles of giant sea anemones which other fish desperately try
to avoid. The anemones secrete a mucus over their tentacles
which prevents them from stinging themselves and the clownfish
acquire their own immunity by gradually covering their bodies
with the same substance. This must be done with the greatest
care and precision. To begin with, the clownfish tentatively
approaches its prospective home and then fleetingly brushes the
tip of a single tentacle with its tail. No harm is inflicted from such
a brief contact and gradually the fish accumulates enough of a
mucus shield to allow it to bathe completely within the anemone.
Such a lethally equipped home has the obvious advantage of
affording the clownfish protection from predators. While feeding
on drifting plankton, they rarely stray more than a metre from
the swaying tentacles in case danger should suddenly threaten.

The clownfish clearly demonstrates the effectiveness of
lodging with another animal, and a similar relationship exists
between certain shrimps and gobies. Inconspicuous against the
sandy bottom of the reef flat, a pair of pale-cream gobies can
sometimes be observed lying motionless next to the entrance of
a burrow. The tunnelled home is not the work of the fish,
however, but of a variety of alpheid shrimp which excavates
grains of sand and fragments of shell using its large bulldozing
pincers. When the burrow is complete, a pair of gobies take up
residence. This might seem to be a rather unfair arrangement
since the gobies have contributed in no way to the industrious
efforts of the shrimp, but in fact the crustacean welcomes its
new lodgers. The gobies have large, slightly upturned eyes which
bulge from the top of their heads rather like the eyes of a frog.
Being bottom-dwellers this enables them to gaze upwards in the
direction of any likely attack. The shrimp, on the other hand, has
poor eyesight and enrols the gobies as its advance warning
system. Whenever the shrimp is foraging for food on the surface
it trails one of its long sensitive antennae across a nearby vigilant
goby which signals danger by darting into the burrow.

Another type of fish has established a niche, not alongside
another creature, but actually inside it. The pearlfish inhabit the

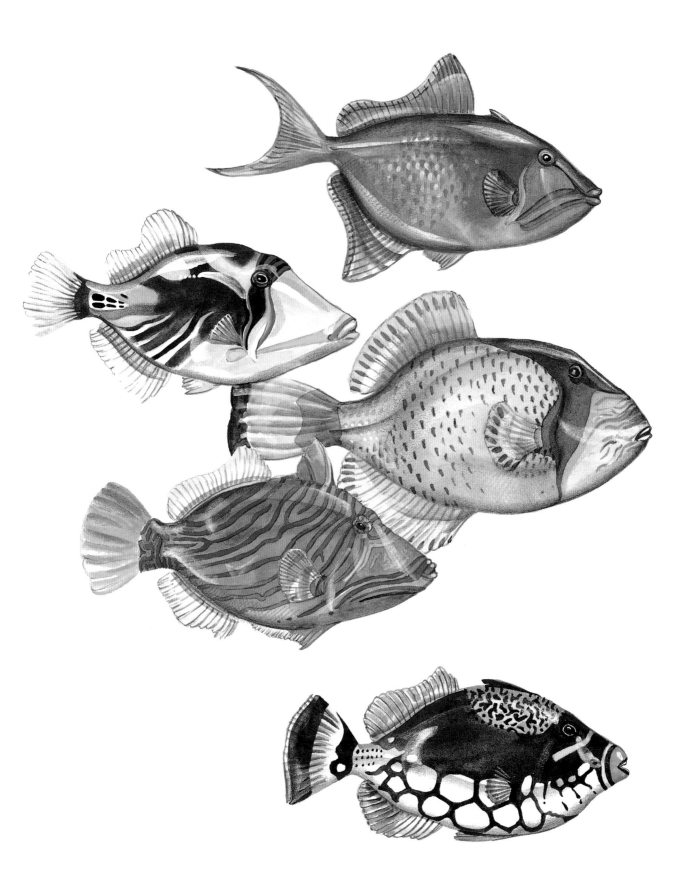

mantle cavities of tropical oysters or the guts of sea cucumbers. Their long slender bodies enable them to slip easily into these living interiors where they remain perfectly hidden by day before emerging to forage under cover of darkness.

Hermit crabs use the discarded remains of animals for a place to live. Unlike other crabs, which grow their own hard outer carapace for protection, hermit crabs have a softer body-covering and carry empty snail shells around with them instead. When threatened, a hermit crab will suddenly withdraw into its shell and seal off the opening with one of its formidable pincers. They are not totally invulnerable, however, since a growing crab must constantly replace its mobile home with progressively larger ones, and during the time it slips out of one shell and puts on another, its soft fleshy abdomen is exposed. If empty gastropod shells are in short supply at a particular location, hermit crabs will engage in frantic struggles to evict individuals from desirable shells. A few very specialized varieties of hermit crab occupy the vacant burrows of coral boring worms. A male and a female live in adjacent tubes and strain plankton from the passing currents using their feathery antennae.

Burrows are a popular choice of shelter for many different reef animals, particularly the marine worms. Some varieties, such as the terebellid worms, burrow into the soft sediment of the reef flat, ejecting a miniature volcano of sand from the entrance. The main body of the worm, which may reach 20cm (8in) in length, remains hidden, but in order to catch food it extends numerous radiating strands of thin tentacles for several metres around its burrow. These sticky, mucus covered filaments snake across the sand surface picking up particles of food before being withdrawn again and wiped over the worm's glandular lips. Other reef-dwelling worms bore directly into corals, secreting acid to dissolve the limestone skeletons of the polyps. Less destructive are the Christmas tree worms which secrete their own tubes on to the surface of a growing coral colony. As new generations of polyps develop and the coral grows outwards, the worms must build their tubes at a similar rate to ensure that their entrances do not become sealed off.

Not all reef creatures are necessarily restricted to such tiny niches in which to live, but the great majority occupy distinct zones of the reef. Different species of triggerfish, for example, live in separate regions to avoid competition for food and space. This is particularly evident on reefs in the Maldives. The Picasso triggerfish is found in lagoons, the orange-lined triggerfish frequents the shallower reef flats, the huge titan triggerfish patrols the reef edge and upper slope, while the boldly patterned clown triggerfish is usually seen at lower levels of the reef slope.

Slow-moving and peaceful creatures, sea horses inhabit sheltered areas of the reef, where they feed on small shrimps and copepods drifting in the plankton. To avoid being swept away in tidal currents a sea horse coils its prehensile tail around a piece of coral, sponge or seagrass, and camouflages itself by developing long weed-like skin filaments and changing its colour to suit its background. Courtship and mating take place over several days and involve numerous intimate embraces between male and female sea horses. Up to two hundred eggs are shed during this period and these are brooded by the male in a special pouch under his tail which secretes a nutritious fluid for the growing embryos. The male pregnancy lasts between two and five weeks before miniature fully-formed sea horses emerge.

Of all the curious partnerships that exist between unrelated creatures of the reef, one of the most fascinating is the cleaning symbiosis between a certain group of small fish and invertebrates and a host of other fish. Over fifty species of fish and a number of invertebrates have found a niche in the crowded coral reef community by offering a cleaning service to its other fish inhabitants. Parasites, mucus, loose scales and lodged scraps of food are picked off and eaten. The most common cleaner fish on Indo-Pacific reefs is the blue, white and black striped cleaner wrasse, while in the Caribbean the neon gobies perform a similar role. The juvenile stages of several species of butterfly fish and angelfish are also cleaners. Most of the invertebrate cleaners are shrimps, including the spectacularly marked Caribbean red-backed shrimp and the Indo-Pacific banded coral shrimp.

All cleaners establish territories or 'cleaning stations' from which to advertise their service. In the case of the cleaner wrasse, this is often a prominent coral head. The wrasse swims with a characteristic

A coral trout opens its mouth and gill covers to allow access to a trio of cleaner wrasse.

■

jerky movement to signal its intentions to potential 'customers'. These may range from a small placid cowfish to a huge predatory coral trout. With rapid efficiency, the wrasse sets to work, darting around its customer's fins and even swimming into its mouth to pick off trapped pieces of food. A hunter resists the urge to swallow an easy meal and instead allows the wrasse further access to its gill chambers, which may also be in need of a clean.

A pair of particularly active cleaner wrasses are capable of servicing nearly two hundred clients in a single hour. Some fish swim considerable distances to cleaning stations where they may have to patiently wait in a queue before being attended to. The cleaning service is obviously an extremely important component in the lives of these reef fish and this is something the sabre-toothed blenny has taken cunning advantage of. The blenny is a perfect mimic of the cleaner wrasse, not only in its identical coloration, but also in the way it swims. It can, therefore, deceive other fish into expecting a cleaning service. But instead of picking away at parasites, the aptly named sabre-toothed blenny bites a chunk of flesh from its unsuspecting customer and then darts away to a pre-planned hiding place.

A fifth variety, known as the red-toothed triggerfish, also inhabits the reef slope, but narrows its range to areas of coral rubble where it lays its eggs in burrows.

Another way of creating some living space is to establish and defend a territory. Several species of butterfly fish, angelfish, pufferfish and wrasse patrol the boundaries of their small patch of reef. Even small damselfish claim territories and aggressively drive away intruders many times their own size – including divers. Only on rare occasions are the belligerent damsels forced to retreat. A fringing reef off the coast of Kenya provided the setting for one such incident. Unwittingly, an octopus had

OPPOSITE
A damselfish hovers above its territory
near the base of a spectacular reef slope
in the Coral Sea.

■

Big-eye trevally patrol the open waters in
front of the reef slope, ever watchful for
an opportunity to dart in and snatch an
unwary fish venturing too far from safety.
Predatory fish launch many of their
attacks at dusk when the light is fading
and their victims can be taken by
surprise.

■

violated the territorial waterspace of a robust dusky-coloured
damselfish. As the octopus glided past with jet-powered
propulsion, trailing its tentacles in a streamlined funnel behind
the bulbous proboscis of its head, the damselfish attacked with a
bullying charge. Undaunted by the irritated fish, the octopus
throbbed through a selection of its guises, changing pattern and
colour in angry succession as it settled into a crevice between
two brain corals. The damselfish darted in too close and a
tentacled arm shot out towards it, guided by the intelligent
vertebrate-like eye of the octopus. The damsel hesitated and
then reconsidered its adversary from a safer distance before
losing interest and swimming away to intercept a multicoloured
moon wrasse.

Although a damselfish will challenge any creature that
enters its territory, the prime purpose of defending its own small
patch of reef is to keep away other damselfish with similar food
requirements. Damsels are largely vegetarian and carefully
cultivate a rich turf of green algae by plucking away other
growths which threaten to overcrowd it. Such choice gardens are
difficult to defend against an advancing shoal of a hundred or
more browsing surgeonfish, but the courageous damselfish is
undeterred by such overwhelming odds and nips at the fins of as
many of the pillagers as possible.

PREDATORS AND PREY

The bluefin jacks had been waiting in the gloom of deep water
beyond the reef and they launched their sudden attack with the
precise accuracy of lethal hunters. The powerful swimmers
covered the short distance to the reef slope in a fraction of a
second and the large shoal of blue chromids, which had been
picking at plankton drifting in the reef currents, were taken
completely by surprise. Instinctively, they retracted into a tight
ball and raced for the sanctuary of coral crevices within the reef,
but the largest jack intercepted the shoal before it could reach
safety. The chromids swerved away from the large streamlined
predator and for a moment they panicked. The dense
impenetrable shoal dissolved into a cascade of glittering blue
bodies as individuals frantically sought avenues of escape. Some
reached the cover of a grove of corals with finger-like growths,
while others raced towards the surface and leapt desperately
into the air in an attempt to throw their pursuers into confusion.
However, more predators were now responding to the
commotion caused by the jacks' surprise attack. Barracuda and
trevally surged into the mêlée of flashing bodies and the
remaining isolated chromids, exhausted and vulnerable, were
snatched in their vice-like jaws. Soon the hunters were drifting

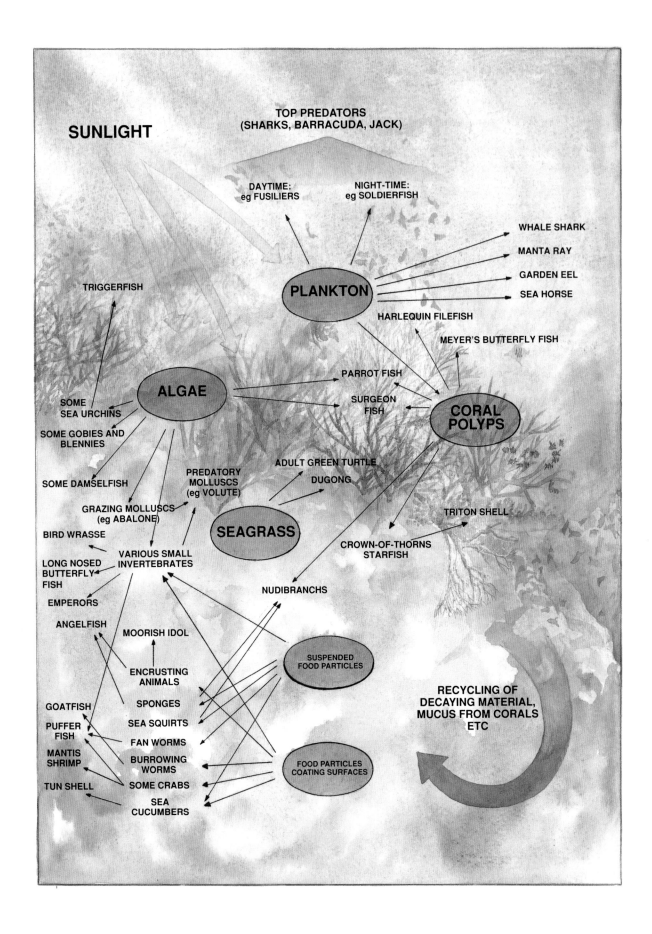

away from the reef, indistinct silhouettes receding into the murky blue of distant water. For a brief moment the reef appeared deserted, but gradually its myriad inhabitants emerged from hiding to resume their foraging.

Two highly desirable options for survival on a coral reef are to have few natural enemies or an effective means of defence. The large predatory jacks and barracuda are among the top hunters in the reef community. They have little to fear and risk nothing by boldly parading in open water. Of all the reef predators, however, the pelagic cruising sharks such as the grey reef and tiger varieties are the most superbly adapted. Successful predation relies on efficient detection and identification of prey, followed by an effective approach and rapid subjugation. The grey reef shark is a lethal exponent of the whole process. It possesses a keen sensory system to locate its prey, a highly powered streamlined body to chase it, and a well-equipped set of jaws to deal with its victim.

Not all reef sharks, however, are fast-swimming hunters. The epaulette shark, for example, is a sluggish bottom-dwelling species which feels its way around the reef flat at night using a pair of sensory barbels located on its snout. These help the shark to find molluscs and crustaceans which are then crushed between its powerful, plate-like teeth.

One of the most bizarre reef predators is the trumpet fish. A deep-gold or silvery-grey in colour, this strange elongated creature has an extended trumpet-shaped snout rather like a giant version of a sea horse. It stalks prey by draping itself over the back of a large pufferfish or parrotfish which it uses as cover. Small fish are unperturbed by the slow-moving pufferfish or the vegetarian parrotfish and make no attempt to flee, seemingly oblivious to the presence of the sinister hitch-hiker. When in range, the trumpet fish streaks out like a fired missile and sucks in as many fish as possible before the shoal scatters in startled panic. After satiating itself the trumpet fish often drifts amongst a clump of long swaying sea whip corals where it hangs vertically.

Some predators do not actively seek out their meals at all, but wait for suitable prey to come to them. Stonefish are by far the most cunning of these surprise attackers. They resemble a rock so faithfully that some species even have fake strands of algae made from their living tissues. Lying motionless amongst a pile of coral debris, a stonefish is rendered virtually invisible. Small fish foraging nearby unwittingly drift in front of a 'rock' from which a pair of eyes stare intently. Suddenly the stonefish lurches forward and with a great heaving convulsion sucks the fish into the gaping chasm of its mouth. After perhaps hours of waiting, the final strike takes less than a hundredth of a second.

The well-camouflaged epaulette shark is a bottom-dwelling species which grows to a length of 1m (39in).

OPPOSITE
The feeding relationships on a coral reef are extremely complex. This food web is a simplified representation of the myriad of interactions that take place.

■

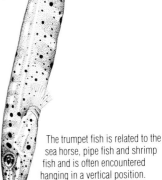

The trumpet fish is related to the sea horse, pipe fish and shrimp fish and is often encountered hanging in a vertical position.

■

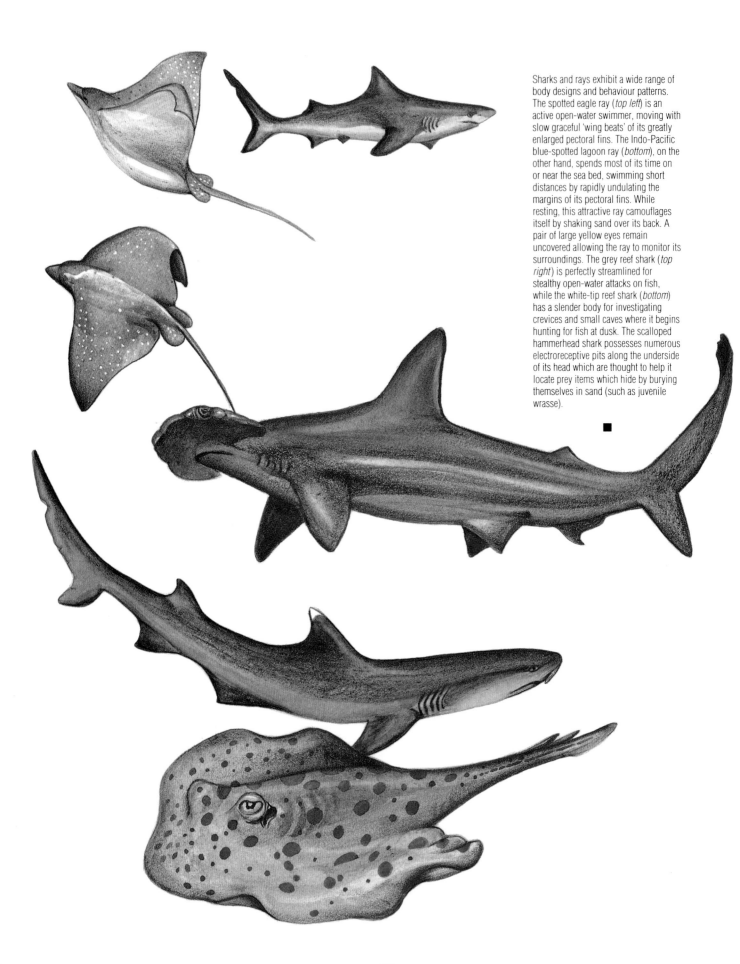

Sharks and rays exhibit a wide range of body designs and behaviour patterns. The spotted eagle ray (*top left*) is an active open-water swimmer, moving with slow graceful 'wing beats' of its greatly enlarged pectoral fins. The Indo-Pacific blue-spotted lagoon ray (*bottom*), on the other hand, spends most of its time on or near the sea bed, swimming short distances by rapidly undulating the margins of its pectoral fins. While resting, this attractive ray camouflages itself by shaking sand over its back. A pair of large yellow eyes remain uncovered allowing the ray to monitor its surroundings. The grey reef shark (*top right*) is perfectly streamlined for stealthy open-water attacks on fish, while the white-tip reef shark (*bottom*) has a slender body for investigating crevices and small caves where it begins hunting for fish at dusk. The scalloped hammerhead shark possesses numerous electroreceptive pits along the underside of its head which are thought to help it locate prey items which hide by burying themselves in sand (such as juvenile wrasse).

Both the trumpet fish and stonefish size up potential prey before attempting to catch it. Anything too small may not be worth giving away their presence for, and a huge mouthful might be too much to cope with. It is a great advantage for a predator to focus its attention on a small range of prey types since it will not only find them more efficiently, but will waste no time continually trying out unpalatable alternatives. The development of these so-called 'search images' helps to avoid over-exploitation of a single type of food on the reef because different predators have evolved unique preferences.

For example, Meyer's butterfly fish feeds on coral polyps, and pairs of these beautiful, ornate fish will search the reef for polyps and nothing else. The threadfin butterfly fish, however, ignores coral polyps and explores crevices for small invertebrates instead. By concentrating on one type of prey, each species has evolved the best way of obtaining it. This explains why the

A stonefish stranded in a small pool on the reef crest by a receding tide erects its highly venomous dorsal spines.

■

The great barracuda, which can reach 2m (6.5ft) in length, is sometimes referred to as the 'wolf of the sea' owing to its reputation for hunting in close shoals or 'packs'.

Surgeonfish have one or more spines on each of their bodies (at the base of their tails) which can be erected for use as scalpel-like weapons when they are threatened or during displays.

threadfin butterfly fish has a longer snout than the Meyer's butterfly fish, ideal for probing for small snails, worms and the like. As its name implies, the long-nosed butterfly fish has an even more elongated proboscis which it uses for winkling out the most deeply hidden crustaceans.

Another advantage of using a search image to locate prey is that it avoids the potentially hazardous occupation of attempting to eat something that is distasteful. Many reef inhabitants distinctively warn would-be predators not to eat them. However, a generalized predator on the look-out for a meal can only learn what tastes good or bad by trial and error. A hungry inexperienced coral trout may well try to swallow a porcupine pufferfish, totally unprepared for its dramatic retaliatory defence mechanism. Before being consumed, the pufferfish rapidly gulps water which massively inflates its body and erects numerous spines from the surface of its skin. What the coral trout had assumed to be a harmless-looking morsel is now a choking spiky ball and the pufferfish is spat out, intact and alive. The coral trout on the other hand now has a sore mouth and makes a mental note never to try and eat a porcupine pufferfish again.

Some species have brightly coloured, highly contrasted markings which serve as a vivid warning that they should not be eaten. A few varieties of non-spiky pufferfish use distinctive patterns to remind inquisitive carnivores that their flesh contains a powerful nerve toxin. One species of non-toxic and readily edible fish called a striped leatherjacket has evolved an identical shape and colour to the distasteful sharp-nosed pufferfish, and is therefore treated with similar respect. How evolution could have produced such a perfect mimic is something of a mystery.

The creatures which possess the most striking warning

The soft-bodied sea hare is remarkably well camouflaged amongst the algae on which it browses. When threatened or attacked, this shell-less mollusc can eject a cloud of dark pigment as an alternative defensive measure.

■

markings of all, however, are undoubtedly the sea slugs, which are also known as the nudibranchs. They have dispensed with a protective shell, characteristic of most other types of mollusc, in favour of an exposed skin riddled with toxins and elaborately coloured to advertise its unpleasant taste. There are thought to be well over 2,500 species of nudibranch and each exhibits a different combination of brilliant colours and dramatic shapes. All nudibranchs are carnivorous, moving across the reef surface on a powerful gliding foot and feeding on sea squirts, sponges, hydroids and anemones as well as the hidden eggs of fishes and other molluscs. Some of the aeolid nudibranchs collect and store the stinging cells from the anemones and jellyfish they devour and then use them for their own protection.

One of the most common means of defence on a coral reef is camouflage; several species blend in with their surroundings and adopt lifestyles which attempt to be as inconspicuous as possible. A tiny crab with serrated edges to its black and white striped carapace merges perfectly with the spines of a sea urchin in which it lives and from which it picks discarded bits of food. Decorator crabs adorn themselves with sponges and algae to

Most sea cucumbers are found on the sandy floor of the reef flat, where they extract plant and animal remains from the sediment. This widespread Indo-Pacific species, however, forages amongst the hard coral framework of the reef itself. Black feeding tentacles with sticky mucus-coated tips ensnare thin layers of food before being retracted to the mouth and wiped clean.

■

There are over one hundred known species of moray eel living in the world's tropical and subtropical seas, the largest of which is found in Queensland waters and grows to over 3.5m (12ft) in length. They display a great variety of colours and markings. Some are a plain olive green, while others are golden yellow with elaborate striped patterns. Moray eels are often found hiding in caves or crevices on the reef with just their heads protruding from the entrance, ready to strike out and seize an unsuspecting fish as it swims past. The eels have wide gaping mouths equipped with sharp fangs which give them a ferocious appearance as they rhythmically gulp water to feed their gills with oxygen. Moray eels will only attack humans if severely provoked or if a diver unwittingly places a hand inside an eel's cave.

obscure their outlines, while several varieties of translucent shrimp become nearly invisible amongst the polyps of some corals. Many types of mollusc have well-camouflaged shells, and even some of the less toxic nudibranchs blend in with their surroundings.

There are also gobies patterned like corals; bottom-dwelling shovel-nose rays and wobbegong sharks freckled like sand; slender shrimp fish which resemble the long spines of the urchins they drift amongst; and a whole array of other fish which mimic sponges and algae.

The cuttlefish and octopus are experts at changing their body tones to merge with different backgrounds, and they do this by controlling the shape and size of thousands of elastic pockets of coloured pigment under their skin. They use camouflage equally effectively when stalking their own prey as they do when hiding from predators. However, these intelligent invertebrates have another defensive trick to play when faced with an emergency. An octopus swimming in open water immediately attracts the hungry interest of reef sharks and trevally and would, at first, seem to be an easy target. However,

as the hunters close in for the kill, they are suddenly confronted by an impenetrable black cloud. Thick sepia ink squirted from the octopus confuses its pursuers and provides ample cover while it escapes using a burst of jet-powered propulsion.

Butterfly fish are also adept at confusing a predator and then taking flight. Several species have complex markings involving dark eye-shaped blotches near the base of their tails or on their dorsal fins and black vertical stripes obscuring their real eyes. A hunter often directs its attack towards the head and is misled into striking at the eye-spot pattern. At worst, the predator harmlessly bites a chunk out of a fin and the vital irreplaceable organs at the other end of the butterfly fish remain unscathed.

This bewildering array of attack and defence strategies is a reflection of the crowded nature of a coral reef. So many animals living close together in a mixed community creates such a demand for food and space that activity on the reef continues for twenty-four hours a day.

The finger-like growths of this coral create an expansive surface area for thousands of individual polyps.

■

FROM DUSK TO DAWN

The spectacular fiery display of a setting sun signals a change in activity on a coral reef. All the herbivorous fish settle down to sleep under coral overhangs or within branching corals. The parrotfish rest on ledges and envelop themselves with protective cocoons of mucus. The daytime shoals of plankton-feeding damselfish and fusiliers nestle within fingers of coral, and butterfly fish move towards designated sleeping spots inside their territories.

As the reef fades into darkness, animals that have been hidden during the day begin to emerge. Spiny lobsters tiptoe out of caves in search of food which they detect with long sensory antennae. Brittle stars, the most active members of the starfish group, crawl rapidly across the surface on five long spidery limbs. Also related to the starfish are the long-spined *Diadema* sea urchins, which appear at night from holes and crevices. They walk across the reef surface at a more leisurely rate than the brittle stars, but use the same system of countless hydraulically-powered tube feet. *Diadema* urchins graze on algae and it is possible they hunt by night to avoid competition from the great shoals of browsing tangs and surgeonfish. Alternatively, it may be to escape the attentions of triggerfish, which are known to eat sea urchins by blowing them upside-down with well-directed jets of water and then crunching through their spineless bases to reach the soft internal organs.

The carnivorous triggerfish may be resting, but the night is not totally without its predators. Lionfish prowl around the coral

During daylight hours nocturnal species such as this soldier fish hide in caves, sometimes forming dense aggregations of several hundred individuals. At dusk the soldier fish emerge to feed on plankton off the reef slope.

OPPOSITE
This starfish is common on the fringing reefs of East Africa. Its brightly coloured skin may serve as a warning to potential predators that the starfish contains distasteful chemicals. A crown of hard conical tubercles also provides a degree of protection.

■

Butterfly fish are one of the largest and most attractive families of reef fish. Illustrated here are (*from top to bottom*) Meyer's butterfly fish, black-backed butterfly fish and threadfin butterfly fish.

At dawn, a small shoal of blue chromids resume their daytime activity, venturing from their nocturnal shelter amongst the branches of a small coral growing in the reef flat.

■

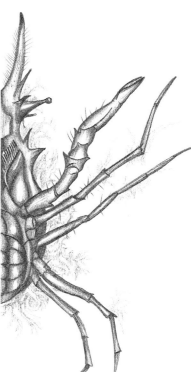

Apart from its protruding stalked eyes, the upper surface of this decorator crab was completely obscured with growths of algae and sponge which the crustacean had placed on its carapace for camouflage. This field sketch shows the underside of the crab.

■

The nudibranchs can be divided into two main groups: the dorids (1—5) and the aeolids (6). The feathery tufts visible on the backs of some of the Great Barrier Reef examples illustrated here are exposed gills. The Sacoglossan sea slug (7) is not a true nudibranch, but belongs to a family of algae-eating molluscs.
(1) *Chromodoris bullocki* (2) *Nembrotha kubaryana* (3) *Ardeadoris egretta*
(4) *Notodoris gardineri* (5) *Chromodoris elisabethina* (6) *Flabellina* (7) *Cyerce nigricans*

gardens flushing small fish from cover and white-tip reef sharks, sluggish by day, become active hunter–scavengers. The most abundant nocturnal hunters, however, are the coral polyps. Most polyp-feeding fish are active during the day, so night is a safe time for the corals to feed (although some soft corals feed during the day). At night, when their symbiotic algal cells can no longer use sunlight to synthesize food, the coral polyps extend their stinging tentacles to catch plankton drifting past.

Plankton is composed of millions of tiny adult creatures such as miniature worms and jellyfish as well as the floating eggs and larvae of much larger reef animals including fish and coral. When darkness falls, other forms of plankton which have been sheltering in hidden depths rise towards the surface to join the hazy, drifting, wriggling hordes already peppering the waters around the reef. All of these creatures are by-products of the reef and while some will be carried away by ocean currents to populate other reefs, many will be recycled back into the ecosystem as food for the corals.

When plankton brushes against the outstretched tentacles of a polyp it automatically triggers numerous stinging cells to fire a battery of poison-tipped threads. These ensnare and paralyse the victim which is then manoeuvred by the tentacles to the polyp's mouth and eventually to a central cavity where it is digested. Beautiful fan-shaped Gorgonian corals grow at right angles to the prevailing reef currents to intercept as much plankton as possible, wafting through their elaborate mesh traps; other corals have large pulsing polyps which create their own food-drawing currents.

Some small nocturnal fish are also plankton feeders: sweepers, cardinal fish, squirrelfish and soldier fish forage in open water relying on the darkness for cover. On some nights, however, truly magnificent plankton-eating fish may be encountered. Manta rays are graceful giants reaching over two tonnes in weight and stretching for 5m (16.5ft) from wing-tip to wing-tip. They feed on the plankton soup simply by opening their gargantuan mouths and cruising in circles near the surface. Water streams in and the plankton is sieved out by special hairy growths on the gills before being swallowed.

Sweeping and somersaulting along the reef slope like gigantic bats, manta rays are attracted to these waters at times when the plankton is especially prolific. On Australia's Great Barrier Reef such occasions may well include the few nights of each year when countless thousands of corals simultaneously shed their eggs into the currents in one colossal spawning frenzy.

CYCLES OF LIFE

It is early summer, and for the past few weeks the waters surrounding the Great Barrier Reef have been warming under the growing heat of a tropical sun. Corals on more than 2,000 reefs have responded to the subtle shift in temperature by making sex cells. Carefully packaged bundles of eggs and sperm are now mature, but millions of unrelated hard and soft corals will not release them until all the factors of a remarkable cueing system are in place. Only when water temperature, light, moon cycle and tidal range are in the correct plan is spawning triggered. On a single summer night following a full moon, the entire Great Barrier Reef becomes the setting for an upside-down blizzard of coral spawn. A parcel of sex cells, jettisoned from each polyp's mouth, floats to the surface and breaks up, releasing a multitude of eggs and sperm. In the resultant cloudy soup, fertilization with another related coral is highly likely and a myriad of juvenile larvae soon develop.

Another annual and synchronized mass spawning event

Each of these small orange structures is a colony of sea squirts. Vast populations of these simple animals are found on coral reefs, where they help to keep the water clear by filtering it. Water is drawn in through the numerous holes located in the body wall and after microscopic food particles have been absorbed, it is ejected through the large central communal opening.

■

takes place around the coral islands of the central Pacific. On a single day in mid-November countless palolo worms begin to break in two, releasing body segments packed with eggs and sperm. These float to the surface and disintegrate, liberating a swarm of sex cells.

Spectacular events such as these provide plankton-eating fish with an overwhelming bonanza of food and their feasting has little impact on the reproductive success of either the corals or the palolo worm. A similar breeding strategy is used by many reef fish, particularly those species which live in shoals off the reef slope. By forming huge spawning aggregations and releasing countless millions of eggs and sperm they strengthen the odds for survival of their progeny.

Other species, such as the blue chromis damselfish, are more particular about where they spawn. A male clears a small space on the floor of the reef flat and then tempts a female down to lay her eggs. The pair then wriggle side by side in the sandy arena, the male fertilizing the eggs as they are deposited. The spawning is still a brief affair, however, and neither parent stays to care for the developing young. Although some butterfly fish form long-term partnerships, they too are poor parents.

A few species of gobies and damselfish defiantly guard their eggs, and clownfish choose a spawning site which is protected by a fold of their anemone. The clownfish also tend their eggs by wafting fresh draughts of oxygen-laden water across them and pick off any dead ones to reduce the risk of contamination. However, once they hatch, the tiny fish larvae are swept away by currents to join the plankton.

Fish larvae are not completely vulnerable to the vagaries of open-water currents. Many have specific behaviour patterns which influence the distance and direction they are carried. Damselfish larvae gather in currents flowing at different speeds and alignments to those occupied by cardinal fish. Surgeonfish larvae travel great distances whereas the fry of some blennies only disperse a few hundred metres from where they hatch.

The larval drifting phase has, therefore, enabled certain species of fish to gradually colonize coral reefs from East Africa to the central Pacific. On the very remote reefs of Hawaii and the coral gardens of the Galapagos Islands, however, fish colonization is slower and less predictable. So far, only one species of angelfish has reached the Galapagos archipelago and in the isolated waters some totally new varieties of reef fish have evolved.

Some sharks invest more time and energy in producing their young. Rather than simply releasing thousands of eggs and sperm, they give birth to live miniature adults which can

OPPOSITE
A sea cucumber stands on end, lifting its body into the path of reef currents where it releases a milky cloud of sex cells from a pore near its head.

■

A highly magnified sample of plankton reveals the tiny floating larval stages of several adult reef inhabitants including the mantis shrimp (1), the crown-of-thorns starfish (3) and the zoea larva of a crab (4). The most abundant component of the zooplankton are often the copepods (2).

■

One population of South Pacific humpback whales congregates in the waters of the Great Barrier Reef between July and October in order to breed. At birth, calves may weigh 1.5 tonnes and reach 5m (16ft) in length. This 15m (50ft) long adult is slapping the surface with its tail flukes.

■

immediately fend for themselves. After a prolonged and sometimes violent chase, male grey reef sharks mate with the larger females and deposit their sperm via a specially modified pair of ventral fins. If the female is not in season she will store the live sperm until her eggs are ready to be fertilized. Between one and six miniature sharks are born after a twelve month gestation period.

Storing sperm is a useful way of making the most of a chance encounter between sharks which are usually both uncommon and antisocial. Fish that live in closely knit colonies, however, are only assured of breeding success if there is a constant supply of reproductive males and females available. Many species have developed a remarkable means of guaranteeing this. They are born as males or females and then change to the opposite sex later in life. All potato cod groupers are born as females and by the time they reach their colossal full-grown size of nearly 2m (6.5ft) they have become functional males. The fairy basslets or *Anthias* which live in large plankton-feeding shoals also change from females to males. They are particularly common hanging off reef slopes in the Red Sea and a single shoal may contain hundreds of small orange females and only a few of the larger mauve males. Parrotfish also undergo a sex change in later life, but perhaps the most spontaneous of all the transsexual reef fish is the cleaner wrasse. These slender blue and white streaked fish live in harems containing a single male and up to sixteen females. Should the male die, or fall victim to a predator, the dominant female of the harem immediately takes on his role, changing into a fully functional male within a few days.

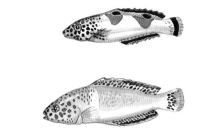

THE REEF FLAT WALK

Snorkelling and scuba diving are not the only ways of experiencing a coral reef. On some reefs, low tide presents an opportunity for a walk across the shallow reef flat. As the turquoise reef-enclosed waters drain with a falling tide, rapids sparkle across the rich coral beds of the reef crest, cascading into clear reef-top pools teeming with fish or being swallowed by dark ocean waves which foam and froth over the reef as it is gradually revealed.

Several reef fish undergo changes in coloration and body shape as they mature. The tiny juvenile phase of the twin-spot wrasse is quite unlike the adult male which may grow to over 1m (39in) in length.

Across the reef flat, a beautiful mosaic of sandy paths and clearings interspersed with outcrops of live coral and dead coral boulders becomes clearly defined as the water surface drops. Some corals of the *Porites* family form circular, flat-topped plateaux called micro-atolls. Like all corals, they are unable to grow beyond the level of low tide. Any growth above this point is rapidly killed by exposure to air and then planed off by wave action. However, the coral does not simply stop growing. It continues to build a skeleton outwards, and over several decades or even centuries, a flat table-sized micro-atoll may develop.

Another type of coral formation that is commonly encountered on the sandy floor of the reef flat is the patch reef. These begin life as broken fragments of coral washed in from the reef crest. If a few polyps are able to survive this ordeal they will begin to establish a new colony and, eventually, a miniature 'reef'. Staghorn corals are particularly suited to forming patch reefs and very often a small shoal of humbug damselfish will take up residence within their branches.

Male and female *Anthias*.

Stepping off the beach of a coral island at low tide into the warm shallows of the reef flat marks the start of what must rank as one of the world's most spectacular walks – wading through a tropical maze, the paths of which are made of soft sand covered by crystal clear water and the walls lined with living coral and

rocky boulders festooned with a dazzling profusion of marine life. The reef walker, privileged enough to enter this maze, is invariably stunned by the cosmos of colours, shapes and textures that can be encountered by examining a single boulder.

Every surface appears to have some kind of algae or animal growing on it. Tufts of emerald-green turtle weed are packed densely amongst translucent clusters of grape weed, while in the gaps fleshy pink anemones have taken hold, together with an array of delicate soft-coral polyps which pulse in a tentacle waving rhythm as they catch food. From the circular entrances to dozens of tiny burrows, Christmas tree worms extend their brightly coloured feathery crowns to trap microscopic food. A clam, with gaping scallop-edged shells, firmly embedded within a boulder, reveals the startling turquoise green of its fleshy mantle. The temptation is always to lean nearer to obtain a closer glimpse of this vibrancy, but a shadow cast across the clam will be sensed by its rows of simple eyes and immediately the shells will close: a defensive measure that guards a potential meal of soft flesh.

Against this colourful background of sedentary plants and animals is an equally spectacular display of mobile creatures. Nudibranchs, washed with delicate hues or emblazoned with bold contrasts of black, yellows and reds, browse on laceworks of orange sponges. A mantis shrimp, some 13cm (5in) long, guards the entrance to its sandy burrow beneath the boulder. Bright green eyes on rotating stalks swivel above a head that conceals folded club-shaped pincers, capable of being spring-released with such force that crabs' carapaces splinter under the impact.

The mosaic pattern of the reef flat is revealed here at Heron Island on the Great Barrier Reef during low tide when the whole region is covered by water that is less than a metre in depth. Circular micro-atolls of the *Porites* coral are interspersed with chunks of coral debris that support a wealth of marine life. One or two sea cucumbers are visible on the sand.

The glossy, domed shells of tiger cowries cruise like giant mobile pearls over the beds of algae, scraping at the plants with rough tongues known as radulas. Other marine snails are carnivores. The murex scours the sandy floor for prey, extracting its victims by drilling holes through their shells. Helmet shells hunt for sea urchins, while the tun shell specializes in eating soft-bodied creatures. Sea cucumbers form a principal part of its diet and these are swallowed whole and then slowly digested. The sausage-shaped Holothurians, or sea cucumbers, litter the sandy substrate in abundance as they gather sediment and extract food from it. Although tun shells seem to be undeterred, the sea cucumbers have a remarkable defensive measure which involves ejecting a mass of ensnaring sticky threads from their gut when disturbed.

Elsewhere amongst the coral boulder debris, the brief slide of a long, patterned body is glimpsed before a moray eel vanishes into one of the infinite number of tunnels, caves and crevices. Measuring a metre or more in length, reticulated morays use

Grape weeds of the *Caulerpa* family of marine algae possess flotation sacs to enable them to float nearer the sunlight above the fronds of their competitors.

OPPOSITE
As the tide ebbs, sea-water drains from the inner reef flat and lagoon regions, flowing over a rich growth of *Acropora* corals on the reef crest.

A reticulated moray eel strikes at a small damselfish that has been flushed from hiding.

■

their sinuous shape to stalk fish through these hiding places. This individual has cornered a small sulphur-yellow angelfish. Carefully, a loop of deadly eel flank surrounds the intended victim. Then, with the tip of its tail, the moray probes for the cowering fish. Large eyes and a gaping mouth equipped with curved fangs wait patiently for the attempt at escape. When the moment comes, the eel strikes with lightning precision and seizes its prey firmly between powerful jaws.

This plethora of life can be viewed on and around any one of the millions of boulders and coral growths that ramify in twisting chains across the reef flat. So intimate is the spectacle, that even the most lavish marine aquarium would be a disappointment following a walk across a reef flat at low tide.

SEAGRASS MEADOWS

On some reef flats a quite different habitat may be found that is dominated not by outcrops of coral but by wide meadows of seagrass. Unlike the green marine algae of the reef, seagrass is a true flowering plant which evolved from terrestrial ancestors about seventy million years ago. It often spreads across extensive areas of sandy reef flat, binding the particles of sand together with a creeping network of underground stems, or rhizomes. These are anchored by roots and bear numerous leafy blades and, occasionally, small clusters of flowers. Threads of pollen released from the male flowers rely on water movements to carry them to receptive female flowers. After the fruits have developed, they disperse in wide-ranging ocean currents which have extended the range of this unusual plant throughout the tropics. The Indian Ocean has particularly abundant seagrass beds around northern Australia and in the coastal waters of Indonesia. Areas of the Caribbean, including the Belize Barrier Reef, also have substantial meadows.

Seagrass meadows support a rich and varied fauna. Worms burrow into the sediment and eject miniature conical mounds of sand, while brittle stars, cushion starfish, sea urchins and conch shells feed on organic matter at the surface. Many of the sea urchins camouflage themselves with a crown of dead seagrass blades and broken pieces of shell. Sea horses cling to the grassy blades with their prehensile tails as they search for tiny particles of food to siphon with their narrow snouts. Large anemones secure their basal discs into the sand and catch small fish with their stinging tentacles. Transparent cleaner shrimps often live in association with these anemones, occupying a similar niche to the clownfish on the coral reef. For the green turtle, the seagrass beds are a source of food.

Just as grass savannas on land support herds of grazing

Upon closer inspection, individual blades of seagrass are found to harbour a variety of life such as growths of algae, tiny anemones and sea squirts, mollusc eggs and juvenile sea horses.

OPPOSITE
A boring clam grows by embedding its shells in the limestone structure of the reef or in a broken and dead piece of coral in the reef flat. It is related to the giant clam, which is reputed to reach over 250kg (550lb) in weight. Both species slightly part their shells to expose a richly coloured fleshy mantle. This contains symbiotic cells of algae which provide the clam with some of its food. Oxygen and plankton bearing currents of water are also drawn in through the mantle via a set of siphons.

■

The mantis shrimp *Odontodactylus scyllarus*, which may grow to over 15cm (6in) in length, is often referred to as a 'smasher' since it possesses a pair of club-shaped appendages (or maxillipeds) used primarily to crack open the hard external shells of prey such as crabs. Other varieties of mantis shrimp are called 'spearers', and use a pair of sharply pointed maxillipeds to impale softer bodied creatures.

Only a dedicated and suitably protected marine biologist would consider trying to handle a mantis shrimp. These beautifully coloured and complex crustacea of the Stomatopod family are well armed and often highly aggressive. Each has a specially modified pair of appendages shaped into clubs or spears which can be spring-released from their folded position with enough force to smash a crab's carapace, shatter aquarium glass or deeply impale the bare palm of a human hand. As the shrimp strikes, a clicking sound is produced like a pistol shot. Mantis shrimps can be found in the shallow waters of the reef flat where they live in burrows under pieces of broken coral debris. They are very territorial, and impressive confrontations take place when one shrimp attempts to evict another from a desirable burrow. The invader approaches the burrow entrance cautiously, with its heavily armoured tail curled under its body and held in front of its head to act as a shield. The resident shrimp waits inside its burrow for the inevitable challenge, and when the two contestants finally meet, a rapid exchange of blows soon follows. The fight lasts only a few seconds; the weaker individual quickly realizes it is outmatched and flees.

mammals, the seagrass meadows have their equivalent in the form of the Indo-Pacific dugongs and the Caribbean manatees, commonly known as sea cows. These gentle slow-moving browsers (which bear a passing resemblance to plump dolphins with blunt snouts) have sensitive and versatile lobed lips which pluck the vast quantities of seagrass necessary for sustaining their large blubber stores. A sea cow's mouth is situated on the underside of its head, allowing easy access to the seagrass. A pair of nostrils, on the other hand, occurs near the top of its head, so the sea cow can take a breath of air at the surface with little effort. When submerged, a flap of skin seals off each nostril like a valve.

Manatees and dugongs are true marine mammals. Their nearest living relatives are the land-based elephants and hyraxes. During prehistoric times the ancestors of all these creatures underwent patterns of evolution which now define their present-day lifestyles. The sea cows evolved forelimbs which could be used as paddles and they took to the sea. In common with other

The milk conch creeps slowly over the sandy reef flats and seagrass beds of the Caribbean. It searches for food by extending a long tube-shaped proboscis into the sand. A pair of stalked eyes are extremely sensitive to large approaching objects, and the conch will rapidly retract into its shell when alarmed.

■

BELOW
Sunlight ripples across the barrel-shaped body of a dugong. The three other remaining species of sea cow (or Sirenians) are restricted to the Caribbean Sea, the River Amazon and coastal regions of West Africa. A close relative of the dugong, the Stellar's sea cow, was eradicated by man from the north Pacific in the eighteenth century. Stellar's sea cow measured up to 8m (26ft) in length – nearly three times the size of an adult dugong – making it an easy target for fishermen. Today, the dugong herds of Australian coastal waters are protected. Only traditional hunting by Aborigines and Torres Strait islanders is permitted.

fully aquatic mammals (the dolphins and whales), sea cows give birth to young under water. The newly born calves are vulnerable and remain with their mother for the first two years of their lives, protected within large family herds that traverse the plains of seagrass.

One of the most important roles of these lush underwater meadows is the refuge they provide for the juvenile stages of many reef inhabitants. Fish, lobsters, shrimps and several other varieties of invertebrate spend the early part of their lives there, only venturing onto the reef when they become adults.

Seagrass beds are also essential in preventing erosion to nearby shorelines. The swaying plains of leafy blades act as a buffer to waves and currents, absorbing their impact. In addition, the subterranean network of stems and roots traps copious quantities of sand (washed in from reefs and created by numerous sand-producing algae that inhabit the seagrass beds) to build protective banks and ridges.

LIFE BETWEEN THE TIDES

RUBBLE DRIFTS

After the sandy reef flat with its patches of coral or beds of seagrass, the islands of rubble that accumulate behind the reef crest appear dull and uninteresting. Dead and broken corals, empty clam shells and the hard cases and skeletons of other reef animals, deposited from wave action eroding the reef, now serve only as clues to the beauty of their original occupants.

Herons use these temporary intertidal islands as staging posts for their fishing forays across the shallow submerged regions of the reef flat at low tide. Pelicans also gather there, occasionally venturing out to sea in bobbing rafts to scoop up water in their voluminous bills before straining it for small fish and squid. Terns and boobies plummet from the skies like fluted arrows, slicing through the water surface onto unsuspecting shoals. Their victims, dangling feebly from sharp beaks, are proudly paraded along the reef crest before being brought to a rubble drift and consumed.

Very few creatures can live on the outer surface of this coral graveyard since it is fully revealed to the hot sun and dry air each low tide, and battered by waves during high tide. Tropical rock oysters, however, are well-adapted to the extreme changes brought about by the tidal cycle. The oyster grows in a fixed position, cementing its shells to a coral boulder so rigidly that only a severe storm would succeed in dislodging it. When submerged, the oyster's shells gape slightly to allow water to flow past its gills, which not only absorb oxygen, but sieve food as well. Unlike the oyster, the limpet has a single shell and this has become flattened and streamlined to offer the least resistance to waves and currents. A strong muscular foot clamps the limpet firmly to a rock and it will only release its grip, to begin grazing on algae, when the turbulent conditions of high tide have passed.

Coral skeletons torn from the reef crest during storms are piled into intertidal drifts. Their outer surfaces are inhabited by only a few animals, which are able to cope with the extreme conditions of high and low tide.

OPPOSITE
On the under-surface of many coral skeletons lying in the rubble drifts is an incredible array of colourful invertebrates. This large plate coral skeleton is completely encrusted with branching growths of pink calcareous algae, yellow and purple mats of colonial sea squirts, as well as sponges and bryozoans of numerous hues.

■

These field illustrations depict some of the creatures that inhabit the beach rock and coral rubble drifts on the Great Barrier Reef. Several types of crab and gastropod are represented as well as the oval-shaped chiton mollusc (with its eggs), a polychaete worm and a barnacle.

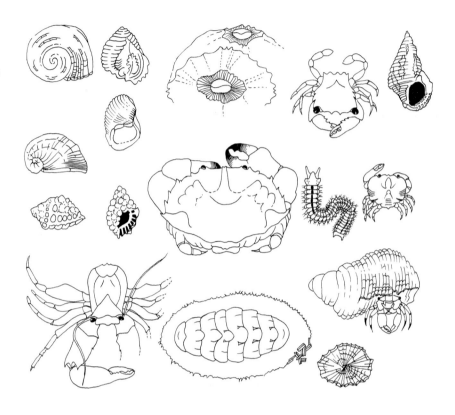

Although hermit crabs usually choose an empty gastropod shell for their home, some individuals have been observed carrying discarded glass jars instead.

Water receding from the rubble drifts signals the emergence of thousands of crabs. Scurrying from their high-tide sanctuary under the protective rims of plate coral skeletons, tiny hermit crabs begin scavenging on the remains of dead animals stranded by the tide. The entire region is scattered with the empty shells of snails and is, therefore, a perfect habitat for hermit crabs, which are dependent on these second-hand homes.

The most abundant forms of life inhabiting the rubble drifts, however, are not immediately apparent to the casual observer. Only by turning over one of the exposed boulders are they revealed. A colourful and diverse micro-world of encrusting sponges, sea squirts, calcareous algae, bryozoans, cowries, sea slugs, worms and a multitude of other invertebrates exploit this hidden niche. The colour is so intense and prolific that one can only conjecture as to its function in a world of darkness beneath a rock. At high tide, while waves pound above them, shelter is the main benefit gained from living in these micro-habitats, but the tides also bring essential food and oxygen-bearing currents of water. At low tide, this world lies hidden from the hot, drying sun in an atmosphere that is cool, dark and moist. It is therefore essential that the boulder is carefully returned to its original position after the spectacle has been viewed.

The corals that flourish at the reef crest rely on strong sunlight and, being marine creatures, this restricts them to a life

in shallow water. At the extreme of a low spring tide, however, this entire region may be exposed and, for a few hours, the corals must endure the burning and dehydrating effects of a tropical sun. Most species are able to provide a good deal of resistance to this by coating themselves with a moisture-trapping mucus. In fact, the most severe threat facing the corals during this vulnerable period is fresh-water, since a short rain squall can spell death for a wide area of coral tissue.

Common inhabitants of the beach rock include hard-shelled molluscs such as this cluster of limpets and winkles.

THE BEACH ROCK

Forming a low rampart between reef flat and coral-sand beach, the beach rock with its eroded surface of pitted depressions and spiked ridges conjures up an image of a crusty lava flow. Many people assume that this band of dark rock is some kind of remnant coral reef but, upon closer inspection, its grainy texture reveals its beach-sand origins.

Many of the animals that inhabit the beach rock demonstrate the same adaptations to high and low tide that are evident at the exposed rubble drifts, further out towards the reef. Relatives of the limpet are found there and they have similarly-designed muscular feet, used for clinging onto the beach rock during the surge of high tide. They include the chiton, a primitive creature with a shell composed of eight overlapping plates, and several varieties of gastropod snail which have more elaborate

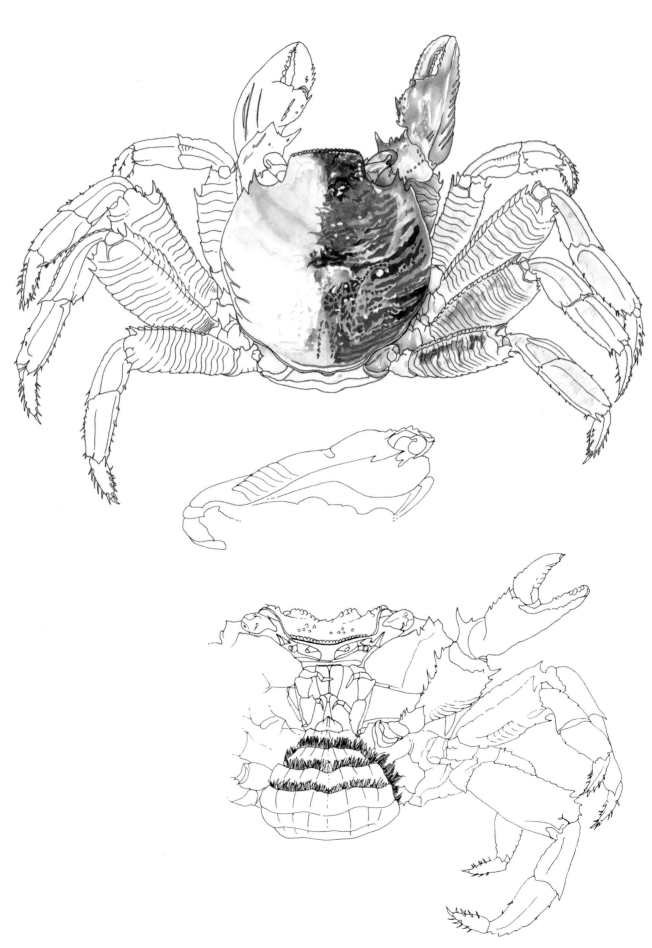

A reef heron stalking fish in the low-tide shallows of the reef flat pauses to take aim with its dagger-shaped bill.

OPPOSITE
A detailed scale drawing of a female swift-footed crab reveals the remarkable complexity of this crustacean's anatomy.

■

coiled shells. Both the chiton and the gastropods graze on a thin felt of green algae which grows on the surface of the beach rock. Much of this feeding activity is nocturnal, as temperatures are cooler at night and there is less risk of dehydration. When low tide coincides with the heat of midday, the chitons take refuge in shaded depressions. Some of the gastropods, on the other hand, have a different means of preventing themselves from overheating and drying out. As if drawn by invisible threads, the snails migrate to form massed congregations of several hundred individuals. These tightly-knit clusters help to trap a film of water which ensures no single snail will dry out.

Gathering in large colonies does have a disadvantage. It acts as a bold advertisement to potential predators. A haunting and high-pitched call signals the arrival of a small flock of oystercatchers. Each black and white bird sports a long vibrantly red bill ideally shaped for prising snugly fitting snails from their shells. The birds hammer the gastropods free with well-aimed blows of their bills. Sometimes a shell splinters and cracks in the process, in which case the oystercatcher simply extracts the soft-bodied snail *in situ*. Other snails have much thicker shells, which may be coarsely ribbed for added protection. The birds take these varieties and securely wedge them upside-down in a beach-rock crevice. The hard plate, or operculum, which a gastropod uses to seal off the aperture to its shell once it has withdrawn, is quickly levered open. Then, with a skilful pivoting twist, the snail is removed and swallowed.

Other birds visit the beach rock in search of different prey. Kingfishers perch on ledges next to tidal pools and plunge on hapless small fish, while a variety of shore-birds, including turnstones, sandpipers and tattlers, patrol the seaward margin of the beach rock (where it merges with the sandy reef flat) probing for buried worms and crustaceans. Perhaps the most skilful of all the hunters in this region, however, is the reef heron. With long legs for wading in shallow water, the heron stalks alone, feeding on fish and the occasional shrimp or crab. Crouching low, with a wing held against the sun to reduce glare on the water surface, the heron carefully watches a shoal of fish that it has herded against the beach rock. Before the fish can seek an avenue of escape the heron lunges with its dagger-shaped bill, snatching a struggling silver body from the water.

The swift-footed crab, a member of the successful Grapsidae family, is a common inhabitant of beach rock and coastal rocky areas throughout much of the tropical Indo-Pacific. As its name implies, this crustacean is extremely sensitive and quickly scuttles to the safety of a hidden crack or tunnel at the slightest sign of danger. Heavy human footsteps vibrating

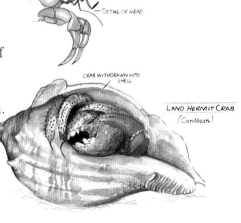

CRAB EMERGING FROM SHELL

DETAIL OF HEAD

CRAB WITHDRAWN INTO SHELL

LAND HERMIT CRAB
(Caribbean)

Land hermit crabs are common on many coral islands throughout the world. These field sketches depict a Caribbean species.

■

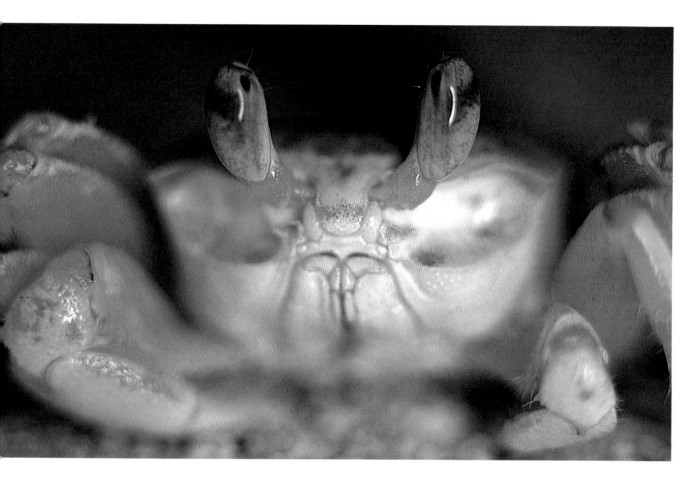

Ghost crabs are common on sandy beaches throughout the tropics. This is the little ghost crab, a particularly fast runner, which will dash to the safety of its burrow when threatened, or failing that, will sprint into an oncoming wave and bury itself in the stirred-up sand within a fraction of a second.

■

through the beach rock cause the crab to take immediate refuge; it is far more rewarding to wait motionless in one small area for a crab to reveal itself. When the crustacean gingerly side-steps out into the sunlight, its elaborately patterned carapace becomes evident. Pale turquoise armour-plating embossed with etchings of dark blue and emerald contrast with the rich mauve of the crab's pincers and its orange-flecked legs. Both sexes may reach 20cm (8in) in width, but the males have larger pincers than the females, which they use for display as well as feeding. The females, on the other hand, have larger abdominal flaps beneath their bodies which are used for storing eggs.

The swift-footed crab is an opportunist, readily accepting a wide range of food that happens to be deposited on the beach rock when the tide drops. Other creatures, such as the small red anemone attached to the lower seaward ridges of the rock, do not have this ability and must wait for a rising tide before they can begin to trap waterborne particles of food.

The swelling tide transforms the beach rock into a dramatic seascape. Great shoals of parrotfish and surgeonfish, swaying in unison with the waves that break above them, move in from the reef flat to browse on algae. Sergeant-major damselfish

A member of the Hydrozoan family, this Portuguese man-of-war possesses an inflated float to harness the sea breeze, but sometimes the wind can play cruel tricks. Most of its long, trailing, stinging tentacles have been lost during the ordeal of being stranded, and this man-of-war's fate will be sealed once the ghost crabs have discovered its whereabouts.

■

investigate the infinite number of small tunnels, while bottom-dwelling rays gather on the sand nearby, waiting for currents to stir up the sediment and reveal hidden morsels of food.

THE SANDY BEACH

The sea gently laps back and forth against the shore, each wave retreating a little further than the last during the subtle transition from high to low tide. The gas-filled float of a Portuguese man-of-war, blown ashore and then stranded by the receding waters, slowly collapses into a pink and blue ooze amongst the broken fragments of sponges and algae on the strand line. Suddenly, a shower of sand explodes from the beach followed by the dramatic appearance of a crab clutching a pincerful of sand against its body. The crab proceeds to scatter the sediment across the beach surface next to its newly excavated burrow. Soon scores of other crabs begin materializing from out of the ground into full view. Unblinking eyes mounted on spring-loaded levers flick upright above spiny carapaces. The beach invaders survey the scene. They have been waiting throughout the high-tide period for the sea to ebb and deposit its strand line bonanza of food. Now, on four pairs of tiptoeing legs,

A land hermit crab twitches its sensitive antennae to detect nearby food.

■

the crabs edge towards the flotsam zone.

Ghost crabs provide a useful scavenging service, eating the dead remains of animals washed in from reef waters, but they are also extremely efficient predators. With an astonishing turn of acceleration, large individuals are able to catch small lizards which stray onto the beach. Insects and spiders are also preyed upon and some ghost crabs have even demonstrated cannibalistic tendencies. During a few weeks of every year, however, certain beaches provide an unprecedented bounty of food in the form of turtle hatchlings. Scuttling frantically towards the sea, thousands of emerging turtles run the gauntlet of the ghost crab zone. Dozens are seized in the crustaceans' powerful pincers before being dragged into burrows and consumed.

Ghost crabs are perfectly suited to their intertidal surroundings. By digging burrows in the sand, they create a sheltered haven at the very margin of the sea to which they return to lay their eggs. When these hatch, the crab larvae drift away in the floating plankton; a few will be destined to emerge as young adults on the shores of another tropical island. This essential link with the sea is evident in other types of crab which spend most of their lives further up the beach.

Land hermit crabs are usually totally nocturnal. During daylight hours they hide under rocks or amongst dune vegetation and leaf-litter. Unlike the ghost crabs, which can lift their lightweight bodies several centimetres above the coral sand and then sprint across its scorched surface even at midday, the hermit crabs with their heavy mollusc shells are slow and cumbersome and would rapidly die from heat exposure if they ventured into the open. Instead, they become increasingly active towards dusk when the sand has cooled. Land hermit crabs are another of the shoreline cleaners, feeding on strand line debris and even the white flesh of fallen and shattered coconuts.

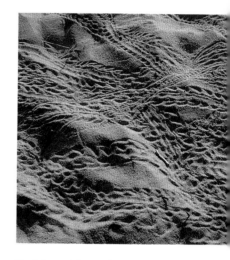

The first rays of dawn sunlight reveal the tracks of numerous land hermit crabs; evidence of their nocturnal wanderings.

■

Another type of land crab is not content to wait for its meal of coconuts to drop from a palm. The robber crab, which can grow to a colossal 50cm (20in) in length, is a tree-climber armed with immense husk-crunching pincers. These are used to cut down the young clusters of coconuts which develop at the base of the palm fronds.

Apart from the various species of crab, life appears to be non-existent on a coral-sand beach and it is true that this habitat may be the least populated in the entire coral reef and coral island environment. However, a large part of the beach fauna is hidden from view. A community of scavenging insects and sand hoppers, for example, lives amongst the tangle of strand line flotsam. Migratory shorebirds such as turnstones and golden plovers wander along the high-tide mark, flicking pieces of sponge, algae and cuttlefish bone aside to reveal this concealed bounty of food morsels.

Nearer the low-tide level, where the sand remains constantly damp, a group of animals with predominantly burrowing lifestyles thrive. Sandy casts ejected from burrows and lying coiled on the surface betray the location of soft-bodied worms. Birds with long slender bills, such as the bar-tailed godwit and the curlew, probe into the sediment and extract these worms along with burrowing molluscs such as bivalves and gastropod snails. On stretches of beach which are sheltered from the effects of strong waves and gnawing currents, small pale-coloured sand anemones root themselves to buried chunks of coral, while periwinkles plough meandering grooves through the wet surface.

TURTLES AND SEALS

On the coral cays of French Frigate Shoals in the Hawaiian Leeward Islands two types of animal, one a reptile, the other a mammal, can be found lying side by side on the beaches. The reptile is a green turtle and the mammal is a Hawaiian monk seal. Both are essentially marine creatures. They have flippers for propelling themselves under water, and a body, particularly in the case of the monk seal, which is streamlined for more efficient swimming. The sea is their larder, providing the seal with fish, and the green turtle with seagrasses and jellyfish. Their link with the land, however, has not been entirely broken. Seals and turtles are the descendants of terrestrial animals and while certain new aspects of their behaviour and anatomy have enabled them to take to the sea, other ancestral traits periodically draw them back to land again.

The first reptiles made a significant evolutionary breakthrough by developing a shelled egg which was watertight and could retain a moist yolk around the growing embryo inside. This allowed them to spread across the land and venture into the driest of places. However, when an ancient group of heavily armoured and cumbersome land tortoises found they could move more freely in water and slowly evolved into marine turtles, the reptilian egg design presented them with a major problem. It was useless if laid in water because the embryo had to obtain its supply of oxygen from the air. So now, when the time comes for a female turtle to lay her eggs, she must forsake the oceans and haul herself onto land.

Several of the world's coral island regions are important nesting sites for turtles. Wreck Island in the Capricorn Bunker Group of the Great Barrier Reef is one of the world's largest rookeries for the loggerhead turtle. Green turtles also nest

After hatching from its subterranean nest, a green turtle struggles free of the sand before embarking on the first stage of a perilous journey to the open sea. A turtle hatchling's view of the demonic looking stalk-eyed ghost crab may well be its last, since these large crustaceans are effective hunters.

■

The last unconfirmed sighting of the Caribbean monk seal was in 1952. The Mediterranean species is now teetering on the brink of extinction, and the Hawaiian monk seal is also extremely endangered.

Hawaiian monk seal.

throughout this group of coral cays, although a greater number make for Raine Island at the northern end of the Great Barrier Reef or the islands of the D'entrecasteaux Reefs in New Caledonia. Several of the islands around New Guinea are visited by green, hawksbill and leatherback turtles. Elsewhere in the Indo-Pacific, turtles nest at the more remote atolls. In the Indian Ocean, for example, there are major rookeries for hawksbill turtles at the Peros Banhos Atoll in the Chagos Islands. Aves Island, lying off the north coast of Venezuela, is an important Caribbean site for the green turtle while Glover's Reef Atoll and Half Moon Cay near Belize are frequented by the green, hawksbill and loggerhead varieties.

The banded sea snake is found in many parts of the Pacific Ocean, spending most of its time in the water and only emerging onto beaches to rest and lay its eggs. True sea snakes, such as the turtle-headed sea snake, give birth to live young at sea. These reptiles are well adapted to a life in water. Their tails are flattened into a rudder shape to provide propulsion when swimming and they feed on a variety of marine creatures such as small fish and their eggs. Sea snakes must, however, swim to the surface in order to breathe. Some coral reef areas such as Ashmore Reef off north-west Australia are noted for their large populations of sea snakes. Divers should be careful not to provoke them since some species, such as the olive sea snake, possess an extremely potent venom.

OPPOSITE
An adult hawksbill turtle swims in the clear reef waters surrounding the Maldive Islands in the Indian Ocean.

■

Turtles have an extraordinarily slow breeding cycle. A female may be fifty years old before she starts breeding. With the onset of the mating season, adult members of both sexes congregate in the shallow waters around coral reefs. Some populations migrate across large stretches of ocean from distant feeding areas. Green turtles that nest on the Great Barrier Reef, for example, swim across 2,000km (1,243 miles) of sea from the waters around the Solomon Islands, New Caledonia and Vanuatu. Once they arrive, the lagoons and reef flats provide a sheltered location where the males can cling to the carapaced backs of the females in a mating embrace that may last for several days. When their role in the breeding cycle is accomplished, the males depart, leaving the females to gather together near selected nesting beaches.

The turtles wait for high tide before embarking on their amphibious landings. During this period, more of the beach is submerged and they can swim with ease across the lower stretches which are exposed at low tide. Eventually they reach the shoreline, where, deprived of buoyant sea-water, each turtle resembles a marooned dome-shaped piece of driftwood. Undeterred by their sudden transformation into heavy, awkward land creatures, they begin to drag themselves further up the beach. Hauling with front flippers and pushing with back ones, heads straining forward, and breathing deeply, the turtles advance inch by inch. The process usually takes place during the night, when the turtles are not exposed to the heat of a tropical sun. At a point where the beach merges with the dunes, above the level of the highest tides, they pause and exhale a ragged sigh. The streams of moisture that flow from their eyes could almost be the tears of endured strain, but in reality they are simply the turtles' way of ridding themselves of excess salt.

After choosing a suitable location, each turtle begins to dig a hole in the sand. With alternate sweeps of the long front flippers a shallow depression is made which is then deepened with ploughing movements of the rear flippers. The eggs are laid in

Eight species of marine turtle are known: the green, hawksbill, black, leatherback, loggerhead, flatback, olive ridley and Kemp's ridley. The green turtle is one of the most common species, found in all tropical and sub-tropical seas. Its head is more blunt and wider than that of the hawksbill turtle, which has a pointed beak and an attractively marked shell of overlapping plates. The leatherback turtle is the largest species, reaching 1.8m (6ft) in length, and is unusual in that it possesses a carapace made of thick leathery skin rather than hard calcareous plates. The loggerhead turtle, so-called for its disproportionately bulky head, is common in the sub-tropics where it breeds. The herbivorous flatback turtle is restricted to the north and east coasts of Australia, while the olive ridley turtle, a carnivorous species, is more widespread in the Indo-Pacific and Atlantic. The only known nesting beaches of the Kemp's ridley turtle are on the Gulf coast of northern Mexico. All turtles are in serious decline as a

Turtle hatchlings have numerous predators including birds such as the reef heron.

result of human pressures such as egg collecting, the marine curio trade, ocean pollution, nesting beach disturbance and drift-net fishing. One of the major problems for effective conservation is to provide protection at each stage of a turtle's life cycle, which often occurs over a wide geographical area.

the pit in rapid streams, several emerging one after the other from a tube-shaped ovipositor, until a hundred or more glistening white, rubbery-shelled eggs have been shed. Sand is then carefully scooped on top of them and patted firm by a flipper.

Exhausted by the night's activity, the turtles head back to the sea and find a submerged ledge on which to sleep. Having only laid the first clutch of the season, they must repeat the entire process another three or four times during the following few weeks. However, when the final batch of eggs has been buried and the turtles return to the sea, they may not breed again for several years.

On islands which are major nesting sites, the number of eggs that are laid in a single breeding season may well exceed several hundred thousand. Many will have been destroyed as turtles returning to lay their second or third batches disturbed existing nests. Another large percentage of the eggs will be sterile. Even so, two to three months after the eggs are laid, thousands of turtle hatchlings begin to emerge from their sandy nest chambers. It is usually night when they hatch, and immediately the miniature turtles head towards the sea, orientating themselves to the shimmering pattern of moonlight cast across the waves. As the first wave of the turtle exodus scurries frantically across the beach, the ghost crabs strike. Many hatchlings fall prey to the powerful crustaceans, but the turtles spill from their nests in such overwhelming numbers that thousands more reach the water's edge unharmed. But even the

sea does not provide them with sanctuary. Shoals of predatory fish have gathered in the reef flat, anticipating this very moment, and the shallows begin to boil as they are driven into a feeding frenzy. As dawn breaks, the stragglers who have lost their way in the sand dunes are easy pickings for daytime hunters such as gulls and herons.

Perhaps only a few hundred turtle hatchlings are successful in crossing the reef crest into deeper, open water and once there, they seem to vanish, swamped by the vastness of the ocean. It is likely they disperse in currents, drifting many hundreds or thousands of kilometres from their birthplace. For the first few days the turtles obtain nourishment from the egg yolk sac they swallowed prior to hatching, and subsequently their food probably consists of tiny jellyfish and other planktonic creatures. The turtles drift in the remote tracts of the oceans for three or four years before moving into shallower regions around islands and at the margins of continents. There, their diets change. The green turtles begin to browse on algae and seagrasses. Hawksbill turtles also feed on algae, but supplement this with sponges, while loggerhead turtles eat molluscs and crustaceans. As developing adults, the turtles continue to be preyed upon. Even fully-grown individuals are consumed by large sharks and killer whales. It has been estimated that of the 1,800 eggs a female green turtle may shed in the course of her life, only three survive to sexual maturity and repeat the cycle.

The Hawaiian monk seal uses a different breeding strategy

A trio of bar-tailed godwits rest at the water's edge on a coral cay on the Great Barrier Reef. These individuals are in non-breeding plumage, but when they migrate to Siberia at the onset of the breeding season, the males will turn a deep rufous brown.

to the turtle. Rather than producing copious eggs which are then abandoned in the hope that a few hatchlings may survive to reach adulthood and breed, the seal invests much time and energy in giving birth to one or two live young which it nurses until they can fend for themselves. Unlike the whales, dolphins and sea cows, which are true marine mammals, the monk seals must return to land in order to give birth. The pups suckle from their mother and grow rapidly on the rich diet of fatty milk. By the time they reach five or six weeks of age, the seal calves are venturing into the sea and learning how to catch fish. Despite their parental care, some calves are still eaten by the tiger sharks and grey reef sharks that patrol the waters.

A dependence on land has resulted in yet another form of predation for both the monk seal and the turtle. Slow and vulnerable when emerging onto beaches to lay eggs, bask or give birth, they have been relentlessly hunted by man.

Coupled with the pressures that monk seals and turtles face from natural predation is the havoc caused by humans. Hunting, egg collecting and ocean pollution have forced many turtle species to the brink of extinction and have left only tiny, faltering populations of monk seals.

THE FRONTIER FORESTS

Mangrove trees possess several ingenious adaptations which enable them to thrive in the intertidal regions of a coral island. One of the most important for this red mangrove is a system of stabilizing prop roots.

Flourishing on sheltered shores, mangroves form a rich and diverse habitat in many coral island regions. The coasts of reef-enclosed high islands may support dense mangrove forests. On the Great Barrier Reef mangroves grow in certain reef flats, particularly in northern reaches, forming the so-called 'complex wooded isles'. Perhaps the best example of mangrove development in reef waters is on the Belize Barrier Reef where there are well over one hundred mangrove cays. These develop on the leeward side of the barrier reef platform where calmer conditions allow the mangroves to become established.

Growing at the very frontier between land and sea, mangroves have evolved a range of adaptations for coping with a life between the tides. Foremost of these is an ability to withstand the salt in sea-water. Some species of mangrove have special membranes covering their roots which prevent the salt from entering. However, most varieties draw in sea-water and then find a way of ridding themselves of the salt at a later stage. A common method involves secreting it from pores or special glands, giving the leaves of many mangroves a shiny, sweaty appearance. Alternatively, salt may be stored in old and dying leaves that are soon to be shed. Other mangroves simply have tissues which are highly salt-tolerant.

Found throughout the tropics, the red mangrove is a

As dead mangrove leaves gradually decay they enrich the deposits of sand that are building up around the mangrove roots with an essential source of nutrients.

The seedlings of the red mangrove germinate while still attached to a mature tree.

pioneer. Supported by arching prop roots it establishes a tenuous existence on a beach or a shallow reef-top where the tidal range is small. The unusual roots have several important functions other than providing stability. Under water they create a complicated woody meshwork which strains the sand and debris from tidal currents. This sediment accumulates as a submerged bank and becomes enriched with the decaying remains of plants and animals swept in from the reef. Dead mangrove leaves are also decomposed by the thriving hordes of marine bacteria which feast on the rotting compost. This concentrated source of nutrients provides the foundation for a successful mangrove swamp. Finely branching systems of nutritive roots spread through the mire, absorbing the organic compounds. A major drawback of this muddy substrate is its lack of oxygen, but this fundamental deficiency is overcome by the aerial roots. By emerging from the trunk or stems of the mangrove, a section of each root will always be exposed to air, allowing vital streams of oxygen to diffuse into the plant tissue.

To ensure the continued build-up of the rich muddy deposits, more sediment-trapping mangrove trees start to grow amongst the tangled roots of established ones. While some arrive as floating fruits from nearby mangrove swamps, others have a rather more extraordinary origin. These seedlings germinate before leaving their parent tree. A small embryonic root emerges from the attached fruit and develops into a long spike. When the seedling is finally shed it either floats away at high tide or automatically plants itself in the fertile substrate at low tide. As sediment accumulates on the seaward side of the red mangrove, new seedlings claim and stabilize it. In this way, the swamp gradually advances further into the shallow waters of the sea. Behind the outer belt of red mangrove, however, other developments take place.

Like the low-lying pioneer beach plants on a sandy coral cay, the red mangrove initiates a sequence of plant succession. By acting as a buffer to strong winds and sea currents, and by trapping sediment to form an enriched mud-flat which is never covered by more than a thin layer of sea-water, the red mangrove encourages less hardy species to settle in the region behind it. A common plant of this inner zone is the black mangrove, which exposes small vertical root extensions (called pneumatophores) above the mud in order to breathe. The succession of various species may continue behind the black mangrove as species with requirements for more stable conditions that are less affected by the tides are able to germinate. On the Belize Barrier Reef, for example, white mangrove and then buttonwood claim the central area of large mature mangrove cays.

Black mangrove trees with small pointed aerial roots dominate the secondary zone of a mangrove island called Twin Cays on the Belize Barrier Reef.

MANGROVE LIFE

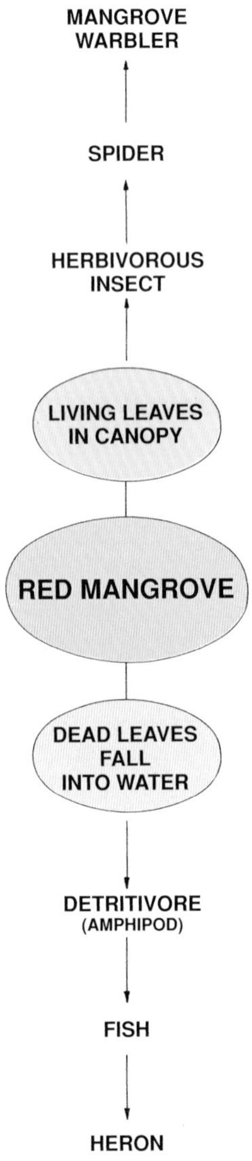

Straddled between sea and shore, the mangrove forest supports a diverse range of animals. Some take up residence in the upper branches of the trees while others inhabit the tidal mud-flats. There is even a wealth of life to be found on and around the prop roots of the red mangrove where they arch into the sea.

Viewed under water, the roots form an eerie world with shafts of sunlight filtering through from the canopy above. Huge shoals of juvenile fish swerve in and out of the woody pillars, glistening with silver as they pass through the rays of light. Like the seagrass beds, mangroves are important nurseries for reef fish. Young lobsters also find shelter amongst the dense root thickets. Occasionally a timid member of the adult coral reef community, such as the awkwardly shaped and slow moving cowfish, finds sanctuary here. All of these creatures are temporary visitors. As the juveniles mature they will start to migrate towards the bustling waters of the coral reef where, as adults, they will fend for themselves.

Other forms of marine life are permanent inhabitants of the mangrove. Covering the surface of every submerged root is a profusion of plants and animals. Orange and purple encrusting sponges grow in lumpy nodules or coat the roots in a smooth skin. Bryozoans smear chequer-board patterns across other sections, while anemones and sea squirts attach themselves in clusters. Several types of marine algae, including the disc-shaped *Halimeda* and grape-like *Caulerpa*, grow in clumps. Corals are non-existent in the mangrove root jungle, for there is insufficient light to sustain them. The waters are also calm and sometimes contain clouds of silt stirred up by the tides. It is an environment quite unlike the clear, wave-swept, oxygen-charged waters of the reef crest and yet, remarkably, the two can exist in close proximity.

As each new aerial root grows down into the water, it rapidly becomes colonized. Space is vigorously contested. Faster-growing sponges either smother their neighbours or grow outwards from the root, swelling into great lobed formations.

The sponges are primitive and simple animals which evolved from the first single-celled life forms over 650 million years ago. They obtain food by filtering sea-water. Their bodies are punctured at regular intervals by small pores, giving their surfaces a cratered appearance. The openings lead through branching tubes to central cavities embedded within them. Tiny vibrating hairs lining the walls of this internal maze draw a current of water in through the pores and then continue to circulate it while microscopic food particles and bacteria are sieved and consumed. The used water is then expelled through

MANGROVE
WARBLER

↑

SPIDER

↑

HERBIVOROUS
INSECT

↑

LIVING LEAVES
IN CANOPY

RED MANGROVE

DEAD LEAVES
FALL
INTO WATER

↓

DETRITIVORE
(AMPHIPOD)

↓

FISH

↓

HERON

A red mangrove tree is the starting point for several food chains, the two most important of which are shown here. Living leaves provide food for browsing insects which are preyed upon by spiders, which, in turn, become prey for insectivorous birds such as the mangrove warbler. Dead leaves initiate another food chain. Less significant food chains are founded on other parts of the mangrove tree. For example, living wood may be killed and partially eaten by wood-boring beetles and their larvae, while a narrow zone of fungi growing on the trunk just above the level of high tide is grazed upon by a type of gastropod.

■

another set of pores. In the star encrusting sponges, these excurrent openings are grouped in small clusters from which numerous canals radiate. It is possible that such an arrangement increases the amount of water passing through the sponge. Indeed some sponges can filter their own volume of sea-water every few seconds – a feat which enables them to tolerate the occasionally murky waters around the mangrove.

The aptly named sea squirts are also filter feeders, but rather than having numerous pores like the sponges, they have two larger funnels. One is used for sucking water and another for blowing it out again after food has been extracted. Some sea squirts are solitary and form a bulbous jelly-like mass, while others are smaller and live in dense colonies. The bryozoans, or sea mats, composed of hundreds of miniscule polyps set in a hard calcareous skin, are always colonial. Each polyp has a set of tentacles covered in waving hairs which channel food-bearing water to its mouth. The general body plan of a sea anemone consists of a single large polyp with stinging tentacles, allowing it to trap much larger prey.

Sponges, sea squirts, bryozoans and anemones are the simplest animal members of this extraordinary marine

A close-up view of a small section of mangrove root reveals a crowded community of purple and orange sponges and translucent brown anemones.

■

117

A colourful and strikingly patterned male fiddler crab ventures from its burrow.

■

Morelet's crocodile is a rare inhabitant of a few mangrove cays on the Belize Barrier Reef.

community. The mangrove oyster is a more advanced creature. By living inside a pair of shells that can be closed together, it frees itself from being wholly restricted to a submerged existence. Water trapped inside the shells will continue to nurture it even if it becomes exposed by a falling tide. This is a major advantage for the mangrove oyster since it is able to live on the sections of root which are revealed each low tide, thus avoiding the risk of being overgrown by the fully aquatic sponges.

Other inhabitants of the mangrove have also managed to adapt to a life partly out of water. Dispersed in the floating plankton as developing larvae, juvenile fiddler crabs are washed onto the mangrove mud-flats. Searching for these timid crustaceans involves waiting for low tide before venturing into the heart of the mangrove swamp.

As you clamber through the red mangrove zone, across a field of slippery arching roots, the shallow waters below gradually diminish as deposits of mud become increasingly thick. The black mangrove begins to predominate, set amongst a glistening mud-flat, riddled with the protruding spikes of breathing roots

and pock-marked with stagnant pools of shallow water. Sheltered from the sea breeze, the sulphurous smell of rotting combined with the heat and humidity are almost overwhelming in the still air. Uncomfortable as the conditions may be for a human, this part of the mangrove swamp is teeming with life and the first animals likely to be seen are the fiddler crabs.

Usually brightly patterned with bold colours, the fiddler crabs appear from their mud burrows at low tide to feed on detritus. They are timid creatures, constantly surveying their surroundings from eyes set on long stalks. At the slightest sign of danger an entire colony will vanish into their individual burrows. When all is clear they move out into the open again, skimming the surface with their pincers and delivering small mud-balls of food to their mouths. Here, the edible components are sorted by a system of twitching hairs and swallowed, leaving a pellet of mud which is discarded. The male fiddler crabs are slower feeders than the females since they only have one pincer that is small enough to convey food to the mouth. The other is greatly enlarged and is used for displaying to female crabs. Different species of male fiddler crab try to attract the attention of females

The arching prop roots of the red mangrove form a tangled woody mesh. Below the surface they provide a niche for a variety of marine species.

in a variety of ways. Some simply twitch their huge pincer from side to side, but others have a more elaborate courtship display which involves waving the claw in the air while jumping up and down, or standing on tiptoe and weaving it in circles above their carapaces. The large pincer may also be used to threaten other males trespassing on a claimed territory, but only very rarely is it wielded in combat.

In many mangrove swamps a curious type of semi-aquatic fish, known as the mudskipper, may be encountered. Using their strong pectoral fins and long supple tails to walk and wriggle across the mud at low tide, mudskippers have solved the problem of how to breathe out of water. Their bulbous heads accommodate a set of large gill chambers in which they carry around their own supply of water. When the oxygen dissolved in each watery mouthful is depleted, the fish return to their shallow pools to collect a fresh supply. While partly submerged in the water, the mudskippers continue to monitor events above the surface using their bulging eyes, which act as periscopes. On the flat stretches of mud, these are also useful for detecting prey.

Mudskippers feed on a wide range of small creatures which live on or in the mud-flat, including juvenile fiddler crabs and worms. Ribbon worms burrow in the sediment or into pieces of decaying wood that have fallen from the mangrove trunks, while polychaete worms, with numerous paddle-like appendages, slither across the surface. Another source of food for the mudskippers falls from the canopy. Tree-dwelling orb spiders spin webs to catch the mosquitoes that breed in the mud-flat pools, and occasionally they drop to the ground where they fall victim to the hungry fish. Stranded flies and wasps are also devoured.

Although the canopy is a rich source of carrion for mudskippers and other scavenging animals such as crabs, worms and snails, it also harbours a threat to them, for roosting and nesting in the dense foliage are herons and other predatory birds.

Several species of shore-bird nest in the mangroves. The striated heron is found throughout the tropics and is a renowned hunter of mudskippers. It is strictly territorial, with breeding pairs constructing their ramshackle nests of twigs in isolation. A more social member of the heron family is the snowy egret which can often be seen in groups amongst Caribbean mangroves, forming a brilliant white contrast to the surrounding greenery. The clapper rail is a resident breeding bird in mangroves of the Greater Antilles as well as several of the Belize Barrier Reef cays. The white, or sacred, ibis, characterized by its bald head and long, downward curving bill, can also be found in those regions,

A Socotra cormorant fans its wings in order to dry them.

■

Mangrove anemones trap tiny, drifting creatures amongst the stinging meshwork of their numerous long tentacles.

■

The upside-down jellyfish is an unusual inhabitant of seagrass meadows and mangrove swamps. It adopts an inverted position on the sea-bed and gently pulses its soft body to create a current of food-bearing water across its tentacles. The tentacles also contain symbiotic algae which provide the jellyfish with an additional form of nourishment when they are pointed towards the sunlit water surface.

■

The majority of tropical sea-birds lay only a single egg, which suggests that the availability of food and the efficiency with which parent birds are able to collect it are insufficient for meeting the needs of more than one chick. Some scientists believe a small clutch is an evolutionary mechanism designed to keep the population below a level where natural resources will not be over-exploited.

but has a wider overall range which encompasses Africa, southern Asia, the northern Great Barrier Reef, New Guinea and the Solomon Islands. Several varieties of kingfisher colonize the mangroves, as do other small birds such as mangrove warblers and finches. All of these birds are attracted to the mangrove swamp both by the shelter it offers their nests and by the abundant supplies of edible creatures that live on the mud-flats, in the surrounding waters, or amongst the canopy.

Many other birds feed further out at sea, but use the mangrove as a roosting or breeding base. They include birds such as cormorants, pelicans and ospreys which are all designed for catching fish in open water. The cormorant swims on the surface, occasionally diving underwater in pursuit of fish. The bird's waterproofed feathers trap a layer of air which not only coats the submarine hunter in a silvery sheen, but also makes it buoyant. Only with strong kicks of its large webbed feet can the cormorant remain submerged for long enough to snatch a fish

with its hooked bill. As soon as it relaxes underwater, it rises rapidly and bobs to the surface like a cork. The oily secretions which provide the waterproofing may increase the effort involved in hunting, but they are essential in preventing the cormorant from becoming waterlogged and drowning.

The osprey has a quite different method of catching fish. Its broad finger-tipped wings are ideal for soaring above the sea, from where its keen, bird-of-prey eyesight can detect fish or squid near the surface. When a likely victim has been identified the osprey swoops down towards it. Spreading its wings to brake and steady the dive, the osprey unfurls its massive talons and swings them forward to snatch its prey. Then, with heavy wing strokes, it carries the prey aloft. Experienced birds execute the entire sequence in a continuous graceful movement. The skin on an osprey's talons is intricately textured with ridges and pits which act like suction cups when pressed around a slippery fish. Once it reaches its nest or a favoured feeding branch, the osprey begins to strip pieces of flesh from its prey using a large viciously hooked bill.

Although the canopy of a red mangrove forest may only reach 4m (13ft) in height, it is often the site for dense nesting colonies of sea-birds. During the breeding season, Man-o-War Cay, a tiny mangrove island on the Belize Barrier Reef, is completely smothered in the nests of magnificent frigatebirds. Approaching the island in a small boat provides a remarkable spectacle. Even at a distance, the swirling specks of frigatebirds can be seen swarming above the mangrove cay, like an agitated hive of bees. Drawing nearer, the cloying odour of the birds' guano drifts past on a sea breeze. Then the stuttered gurgling clamour of their voices begins to rise and fall with the currents of air. A few individuals stream away from the island, gliding effortlessly on long slender wings swept back to rakish points. Frigatebirds are the ultimate flying machines. They never walk or swim if they can possibly avoid it. Each subtle nuance of their posture, every angle and shape in their design, from the fluted outer tail feathers to the long streamlined bill, conveys the essence of flight. Overhead, two frigatebirds pirouette, calmly embracing a nudge of wind before drifting back to the island.

Male frigatebirds build a rudimentary nest of twigs amongst the branches of the mangrove before turning their attention skywards to where potential mates are gliding back and forth. The males then begin an extraordinary courtship display. Firstly, they must inflate a small wrinkled pouch of bare skin beneath their throats into a huge red balloon. When a female flies past, the males lift their heads and send quivering vibrations through the rosy air-filled sacs. Any show of interest from a female

It is on low, wooded, isles that mangrove communities form an integral part of the Great Barrier Reef. They are found in the northern reaches of the Reef, including regions such as Low Isles near Port Douglas. A sand cay develops on the leeward side of a coral reef and on the windward side a bank of shingle accumulates. Mangrove trees then colonize the sheltered depression lying between the two. Low Isles is an important breeding site for several species of sea-bird and was also the location of the Great Barrier Reef Expedition which took place between 1928 and 1929. This was one of the first significant pieces of scientific research to be carried out on coral reefs and did a great deal to advance the current knowledge of reef, mangrove and seagrass communities.

frigatebird sends the male into a head weaving, bill snapping frenzy. His throat pouch swells to near bursting point amidst gabbled outbreaks of warbling 'wah-ho-hos'. Male frigatebirds put a tremendous amount of effort into their ceremonial displays and eventually pairs become established. Both birds complete the construction of the nest, occasionally pausing to rattle their bills together as if confirming their commitment to breed together.

A single glossy white egg is laid and the parents take turns to incubate it over the following fifty or so days. The chick is naked when it hatches, but soon becomes a round fluffy ball with a smaller version of the adults' long hook-tipped bill protruding from the mass of white down. The hatchling has a voracious appetite, but the parents are accomplished hunters.

Squid, flying fish and other surface-living prey are plucked from the water. Patrolling beaches, frigatebirds are quick to swoop on crabs and hatchling turtles and have even been known to steal eggs from other sea-birds' nests. Of all the methods of

Magnificent frigatebirds soar above their nests in the mangroves of Man-o-War Cay.

ABOVE LEFT
A male magnificent frigatebird with red throat sac fully inflated.

■

hunting, however, one particular technique has given rise to the frigatebird's alternative names of sea hawk or man-of-war bird: the frigatebird is a pirate.

Hanging high above the sea on a billowing column of rising air, a lone frigatebird waits for its victim. The glittering pattern of sunlit waves is distracting and the red-footed booby, flying low and fast, almost reaches the sanctuary of its nest hidden in the mangrove canopy; but the sea hawk has spotted it. Outspread wings fold slightly, spilling the buoyant air from beneath them, as the frigatebird pitches forward into a spectacular dive. The booby senses the impending attack and swerves desperately, but the movement is awkward. The frigatebird stalls and then twists neatly alongside the booby, buffeting against it. Submitting to its determined harasser, the booby regurgitates its crop of fish and the frigatebird catches the partly digested food in mid-air. The piratized meal will be welcomed by its hungry chick.

125

ISLAND WORLDS

THE ISLAND OF BIRDS

The coastline of Atiu is magnificently rugged. Sheer cliffs of fossil coral, reaching 18m (60ft) in height in some places, rise from the shallow waters surrounding this raised reef island. Since Atiu's original fringing reef was forced out of the sea to form a kilometre-wide coastal plateau known as the *makatea*, a new coral reef has begun growing around its perimeter. Ocean waves curl against the reef and then topple forward, gushing over the narrow reef flat and colliding with the sheer edge of the makatea with such force that spray erupts in great fountains after each impact. Over the years, the sea has gnawed away the base of the cliffs, and continues to undercut them with its biting waves.

On the surface of the makatea, other forms of erosion are taking place. A virtually impenetrable jungle of ferns and trees has taken hold, shattering the ancient coral limestone with its questing roots. Wind and rain have scoured the surface into a relief of razor-sharp ridges. Pockets of rain-water, acidified by a leaching layer of humus, have cut deeply into the makatea, dissolving the alkaline limestone and carving subterranean passages. In some locations, the underground erosion has been so extensive that large caverns have been created. The entrances to these mysterious caves, obscured by trailing curtains of vines, are hidden in the densely vegetated heart of the makatea. Only the native Cook Islanders, who inhabit Atiu, know how to find the makatea caves. They buried their ancestors in some of them, but one cave, known as Ana-taki-taki, is special for another reason; living in its deepest chamber are the *kopeka*, and they are found nowhere else in the world.

To reach the Cave of the Kopeka involves scrambling across a wide section of the forest-clad makatea. At some points, great blocks of fossil coral form narrow canyons, and in others the

Portrait of a white reef heron.

OPPOSITE
Deep blue South Pacific waters encircle the island of Atiu in a foaming wreath of surf. This aerial view shows the makatea; a coastal plateau created by the upheaval of a former coral reef, which has since been colonized by a forest of trees and ferns.

127

barely discernible path is totally clogged with vine tendrils. Huge blue land crabs scuttle into the undergrowth, backing into crevices with their formidable pincers splayed wide in a defensive posture. Bronze-coloured skinks freeze on tree trunks. Occasionally, a fluttering sound betrays the presence of a rare Cook Islands fruit dove, but otherwise, the makatea is an unearthly and quiet world. A few metres ahead, a chink in the forest canopy focuses a shaft of light through emerald-dappled leaves and then vanishes into a dark hole – the mouth of Ana-taki-taki.

Climbing down into the cave, a narrow passage leads into a large open-sided cavern. Honey bees drone around their hive at the summit of a steep rock face. Atiuan honey from the makatea bees is regularly collected by the islanders. The next chamber is more extensive, with numerous stalactites and stalagmites piercing the roof and floor and sometimes merging to form thick pillars of rippling limestone. After a hundred metres this cavern becomes engulfed by darkness and silence. Suddenly, the stillness is broken by the echoing call of a kopeka. A beam of torchlight reveals a fluttering shadow whirring past the pale cathedral sculptures of limestone, accompanied by a rapid clicking sound.

The kopeka are tiny brown cave swiftlets, and their call enables them to fly with confidence inside caves by using a technique known as echolocation. Each click pulses into the cave and rebounds off any obstacles (such as stalactites) lying in the swiftlet's flightpath. The speed at which the echo returns informs the bird how close the looming obstacle is. As the kopeka fly towards the cave opening, their clicks become less frequent as normal daylight vision replaces echolocation. Once outside, the swiftlets hunt for flying insects high above the island.

Atiuan cave swiftlets build their nests on the roof of the coral limestone cave. The bird dribbles its saliva onto strands of plant material collected from the makatea forest. This solidifies into a pale brittle substance which is gradually built up in layers to form a tiny bracket-shaped cup, glued to the high rock ceiling. A single egg is laid and when the hatchling emerges it is totally naked. Crouching in its precarious nest, the young swiftlet waits for its parents to return with food. The ability of the adult birds to navigate to the precise location of their nest is quite remarkable.

Atiu's Cook Islands' name is *Enua Manu*, meaning 'Island of Birds', a reference to its unique cave swiftlets. However, several other species of land-bird inhabit the island's undisturbed makatea forest. As well as the Cook Islands fruit dove, there are populations of Pacific pigeons and long-tailed cuckoos. On the

A cave swiftlet, or *kopeka* as they are known on the island of Atiu.

Spectacular limestone formations adorn a mysterious cavern hidden deep within the makatea of Atiu in the Cook Islands.

■

The megapodes are an unusual family of birds which resemble small, darkly coloured guinea fowl. They bury their eggs within rotting piles of vegetation, in dark-coloured sand or even near the active vents of volcanoes. All of these locations provide ample warmth for incubating the eggs, relieving the parents of the vulnerable and potentially hazardous occupation of sitting on a nest. Megapodes are widespread in south-east Asia, New Guinea and northern Australia. There are also isolated populations in Micronesia and on the Solomon Islands, Vanuatu and Niuafo'ou in Tonga. The remains of other island species, including a family of giant varieties, have been discovered in many areas of the Pacific Ocean. They were probably hunted to extinction following the arrival of man. Today, the Pacific islanders attempt to harvest megapodes' eggs on a sustainable basis, but there are signs that some populations are declining.

Heron Island, viewed here from the reef crest at low tide, is an important nesting location for black noddies and wedge-tailed shearwaters.

inside edge of the makatea is a lowland swampy region, which at one point gives rise to a small lake inhabited by wild ducks and frequented by kingfishers and egrets. Wandering tattlers, visiting Atiu as part of their annual migration, wade through the shallows feeding on small worms buried in the mud. The lake is connected to the sea by an underground tunnel and breathes with the tides. Dense vegetation, including trees of the widespread Pacific *Metrosideros*, crowds its margins. White terns, renowned for balancing their eggs on branches, fly amongst the trees with dainty flicks of their wings. High above the canopy, frigatebirds drift on ocean winds, their dark angular shapes contrasting with the blue tropical sky. Red-tailed tropicbirds swirl around them, trailing their long streaming tail feathers. The tropicbirds nest on a small coral cay called Takutea, lying to the north of Atiu.

The birdlife is often the most conspicuous fauna on a coral island. Many islands in the world's tropical seas support

populations of warblers, flycatchers, doves, kingfishers, rails and other land-birds. Many types of migratory bird, particularly wading species which breed near the Arctic, overwinter on coral islands. Other shore-birds, such as herons and oystercatchers, are resident all year round. The ocean-travelling sea-birds, including terns, noddies, boobies, frigatebirds, tropicbirds and shearwaters, are often the most abundant members of the island bird community, particularly during the breeding season when they arrive to nest. One of the most important breeding environments for a wide variety of species are the coral cays, for they provide a small, isolated sanctuary for nesting which is usually devoid of mainland predators and is surrounded by sea containing abundant food.

REALM OF THE SEA–BIRDS

It is the start of the breeding season on Heron Island, a forested coral cay lying in the Capricorn Group of the Great Barrier Reef.

In the cool stillness of early dawn, the first tentative rays of sunlight steal across the dunes, casting a soft wash of light across low-lying grasses and glistening on dew-laden spiders' webs. Gradually, as the sun climbs higher, shafts of brighter light reach into the denser growth of the forest, spotlighting a patch of thick orange leaf-litter or toning a dark shadow with the subtle blend of tans and ochres of a tree trunk. A faint whisp of ocean breeze nudges the dune-covered grasses and carries the sound of reef surf to the coral cay. Occasionally a black noddy utters a throaty squawk from a branch in the woodland or forest. Most of the other noddies that inhabit this coral island are swirling over the reef waters, revelling in the new light as they swoop on small fish, squid and jellyfish, plucking them from the surface with deft swipes of their long slender bills. The wedge-tailed shearwaters have also left the island, under cover of pre-dawn darkness. They will fish further out at sea and not return until dusk.

For now, however, the birds that remain on the coral cay herald the sunrise with their song. Silvereyes warble and pipe to an accompaniment of whistling sacred kingfishers and cooing bar-shouldered doves. As some of the noddies begin to return to their nests in the woodland and forest, their range of clicks, gurgles and croaks is added to the chorus. The reef herons become infected by the rising orchestra of bird calls and join in with deep-throated baritone coughs.

Early morning sunlight penetrates the *Pisonia* forest on Heron Island.

■

While the cay is laced in a veil of moist dew, and before the tropical sun of mid-morning has evaporated it, several pairs of black noddies are seized by an urge to collect nest material; it is likely that the dead leaves of *Pisonia* trees are easier to fix in place when they are damp with early-morning dew. One bird frantically dives and wheels, snatching a leaf from the ground and presenting it, with much friendly nodding, to its partner perching on the existing nest. The leaf is tested by the nest builder for size and shape and is invariably rejected and allowed to float to the ground. Tenaciously, the partner dives to catch it and once more hands over the donation. The antics of noddy nest-building continue amidst a growing clamour of noises, foremost of which are the frustrated cries of leaf-collecting noddies gathering up their rejected leaves. The completed nest is a shallow cup of leaves interwoven with marine algae and grass, and cemented together with the birds' droppings.

The black noddy is found in the tropical regions of the Pacific and Atlantic Oceans where it nests amongst trees in densely packed colonies. Its larger relative, the brown noddy, is a more widespread species, breeding on islands throughout the tropics. The brown noddy constructs a simple nest on the ground, usually consisting of a shallow hollow in the sand lined

The pied oystercatcher usually lays its eggs in a shallow scrape well above the high-water mark. Although well camouflaged amongst the strand line, this clutch risks being swamped by waves at high tide.

OPPOSITE
A few dead leaves have been gathered by this pair of black noddies to form the foundation of their nest.

■

with sticks, marine algae and small pieces of coral.

Sea-birds demonstrate a remarkable variation in the location and structure of their nests. This may be an adaptation for avoiding competition over space, which is a precious commodity on a small coral island, particularly as some sea-birds nest in such large colonies. The boobies (or tropical gannets) are, like the brown noddy, circumtropical, and two or three different species often nest on the same coral island. Each, however, has quite different nesting habits. The red-footed booby builds a nest of twigs in a tree or shrub; the masked booby digs a shallow scrape in open ground; and the brown booby chooses a site on the ground that is screened by bushes.

The majority of terns are also ground nesters, laying their solitary eggs in sandy depressions. Some species, such as the crested tern, prefer ground that has a covering of low-lying pioneer plants. The lesser-crested and black-naped terns, on the other hand, are content with bare sand – as long as it lies above the high-tide mark.

Another family of sea-birds that show little interest in gathering material to build or line a nest are the tropicbirds. The white-tailed tropicbird breeds on islands in most tropical seas and lays its egg in a crevice amongst coral rubble, or under a rocky overhang on larger volcanic islands. It has even been known to deposit an egg in the fork of a tree. The Indo-Pacific red-tailed tropicbird digs a shallow scrape on the ground, sheltered by a rock or bush.

Shearwaters and some petrels exert far more effort in the nesting process. Labouring away for several hours at a time, they dig long burrows in the sand.

All of these different nesting techniques can be related to the state of plant succession on a coral cay. A young unvegetated cay in the Indo-Pacific will attract bare-ground-nesting sea-birds such as masked boobies and black-naped terns. As pioneer plants become established, crested terns may begin to nest. The sequence could culminate with tree-nesting black noddies and great frigatebirds breeding amongst the climax forest vegetation.

Although Heron Island consists of little more than a single square kilometre of land, it supports a population of over eighty thousand black noddies. Every octopus bush and *Pisonia* tree is host to numerous nests, and each leaf and branch bears the splattered white of their guano, permeating the island with its rich and exotically pungent scent. Adjacent nests are sometimes so close together that fights break out as one bird is caught in the act of stealing a leaf from its neighbour's nest. As the debate becomes more heated, the sparring pair often crash to the ground and grapple with each other in various wrestling holds.

Field sketches of various terns observed at their roost amongst a pile of coral rubble on a Great Barrier Reef coral island.

Domestic squabbles are a common feature of dense sea-bird colonies, but the advantages of living close together in large numbers far outweigh such hardships. An approaching predator, for example, is likely to be noticed by at least one individual in a colony of several thousand, whereas the predator may well launch a surprise attack on a solitarily nesting bird.

The white-breasted sea eagle, although renowned for its spectacular method of snatching fish from the sea, is also a hunter of other sea-birds' nestlings. Occasionally, an eagle visits Heron Island. Soaring low over the *Pisonia* forest it causes an uproar amongst the black noddies. Only a few of the noddies glimpse the eagle as it passes overhead, but their alarm calls rapidly alert the rest of the colony to its presence. Several hundred noddies rise in a swirling vortex towards the bird of prey, harassing it in such numbers that it is forced to flee across the reef flat.

Many coral islands, which are either bare sand or covered with low-lying grasses, are inundated with thousands of ground-nesting sea-birds at the onset of the breeding season. The most conspicuous species are often terns. The sooty tern nests on islands everywhere within the tropics, usually in huge colonies. On the Great Barrier Reef, more than twenty thousand nest on Michaelmas Cay (along with fourteen other species), and the atolls of the Phoenix and Line Islands support breeding populations of several million. The Chagos Islands and Cargados Carajos Shoals (near Mauritius) in the Indian Ocean are also renowned nesting sites for sooty terns, as are the cays in the Bahamas and the Alacran Atoll near Mexico.

A pair of white-breasted sea eagles used to nest on each of the vegetated Capricorn Islands of the Great Barrier Reef, returning generation after generation to traditional breeding sites. Human disturbance has now led to fewer pairs, but the eyrie at One Tree Island, reported to exist by the naturalist aboard HMS *Fly* in 1843, is still in use. This one year old juvenile will acquire a black, white and slate-grey plumage of an adult in three years' time. The parents have already banished the youngster from their breeding and hunting territory and until this individual finds a mate and a territory of its own, it will remain a vagrant. Sea eagles prey on fish, squid, sea snakes and nestlings, but will also scavenge on carrion.

■

The collection of certain shells is banned in some countries. The giant triton and horned helmet shell, for example, are not allowed to be collected in Fiji, Indonesia or Australia, and similar controls exist for the imperial harp shell in Mauritius.

Other sea-birds have a far more restricted breeding range. One species of frigatebird, for example, is found only on Christmas Island in the Indian Ocean. Similarly, the black-capped petrel breeds in a small part of the Caribbean Sea around Hispaniola.

The Laysan and black-footed albatrosses only nest on a few remote islands in the north Pacific Ocean. The adults spend four or five months of every year soaring above the vast watery tracts of the ocean, without ever making landfall, before navigating towards two tiny coral cays at Midway Atoll in the Hawaiian Leeward Islands. Over half a million Laysan albatrosses (more than a third of their entire world population), and smaller numbers of the black-footed albatross, arrive on the islands to breed. Elaborate ritual dances and mutual preening reinforce the bond between pairs that will mate for life. Standing opposite each other, the male and female rattle their large robust bills together, bob their sleek white heads up and down and drum their webbed feet on the ground. The courtship dance is

complicated, but beautifully synchronized and is accompanied by a wide range of rasping calls and clapping sounds.

Many types of sea-bird proclaim and reinforce the bond with their breeding partners through nest-side courtship rituals. Boobies raise their heads and tails and fan their wings, noddies nod and croon, and petrels rattle bills and preen one another. A tern presents its mate with a small gift of fish, after which the pair take to the wing, twisting around each other in an aerial courtship display. Tropicbirds also take part in spectacular courting flights. Calling to each other, pairs soar upwards, with tail streamers rippling, before stalling into a fluttering hover and swooping away.

Courtship sometimes includes symbolic nest building. The male Laysan albatross collects a few pieces of grass and twigs and presents them to the female. She accepts them as a token of his sincere intentions to be her mate. Once the insubstantial symbolic nest is completed, however, it is left entirely to the female to construct a functional one that will contain her egg. A bowl shaped mound of sand and plant material is gathered together, and while one parent broods the egg, the other glides over nearby waters, catching squid. After the chick has hatched it grows rapidly, feeding on regurgitated food from its parents.

By late July, the albatross colony is crowded with fully fledged juveniles, eager to take to the wing. Short practice flights

Elegant black-naped terns, tinged pink with breeding plumage, take to flight from an area of coral rubble. Black-naped terns nest on coral islands throughout the Indian and western Pacific Oceans.

ABOVE RIGHT
A pair of courting black-naped terns.

■

take place along the beach where a sea breeze provides enough uplift for these giants of the sea-bird world. Landing skills are also developed. Frantically back-flapping with its wings, an airborne albatross uses its fanned tail and webbed feet, held out below, as air brakes. Many of the inexperienced juveniles crash-land in the sea and this is when the tiger sharks strike, dragging the wallowing birds beneath the surface. By some remarkable instinct, the sharks know when the Laysan albatrosses begin to leave their nesting islands, and large numbers gather in the surrounding waters in anticipation.

It has long been thought that adult tropical sea-birds have few natural enemies. Their chicks often fall prey to frigatebirds and gulls, and occasionally juveniles are taken by sea eagles or even sharks. Threats to adults, however, seemed to be rare, until, that is, a masked booby was discovered inside the stomach of a large grouper. Many sea-birds dive underwater to catch their prey of fish and squid. A flock of boobies rocketing into the water as they plunge-dive for fish is a memorable sight, but the birds can only dive to a relatively shallow depth, and feed mainly on shoals near the surface. Perhaps unknown to them is the fact that these shoals are often driven to the surface by large predatory fish attacking from below. As the sea-birds streak under the surface, they come face to face with their marine competitors, sometimes with painful or fatal consequences.

During the last ice age, the limestone bedrock of the Belize Barrier Reef was exposed and caves and sink holes were eroded into its surface. Around 7,000 years ago, these were flooded by rising sea levels to form underwater caverns and 'blue holes' where divers can now explore prehistoric stalactite and stalagmite formations. One of the most famous is The Blue Hole at Lighthouse Reef which was studied by Jacques Cousteau.

Sea-birds demonstrate a variety of fishing techniques. From top to bottom: the magnificent frigatebird robs other birds of their meals or plucks squid and flying fish from the surface, whereas the booby dives on shoals of fish. The cormorant swims on the surface, ducking underwater in pursuit of its prey.

Portraits of a little pied cormorant, brown booby, white-throated storm petrel and Laysan albatross.

■

Petrels (of the non-diving family) and storm petrels are more reluctant to enter the water in their pursuit of prey. The petrels skim low over the sea, occasionally dipping for fish, whereas the dainty little storm petrels flutter near the surface, dabbling their webbed feet in the water as they pick tiny squid and crustacea from the plankton.

Several species of petrel (including Murphy's, Gould's and the Kermadec petrel) breed on islands in the central and southern tropical regions of the Pacific Ocean. The Tahiti and herald petrels nest on South Pacific islands west of the Marquesas group and are also found at Mauritius and Reunion in the Indian Ocean. The white-throated storm petrel is widespread in the central Pacific Ocean, and as recently as 1989 a new species of storm petrel was discovered breeding in the Austral Islands south of Tahiti by leading ornithologist Peter Harrison.

Petrels, storm petrels and shearwaters are smaller relatives of the albatrosses and all of these beautiful ocean wanderers are classified under the unflattering heading of tube-nosed sea-birds. Many possess prominent tubular nostrils located on the top mandible of their bills. These give the birds a keen sense of smell which, coupled with their strong musky odours, helps them to locate their individual nests in the midst of a crowded breeding colony. The wedge-tailed shearwater, which only returns to its nesting island after sunset, must find this a great advantage.

As dusk falls over Heron Island, all that remains of the sun is an orange smear on the horizon, but in its glow the silhouettes of noddies can be glimpsed flying in closely paired formations and making a strange clicking sound in time with the frequency of their rapidly beating wings. One by one, amongst the noddies, other birds appear. Silently and on long pointed wings, these bigger arrivals soar and slice through the deepening dusk with an effortless mastery of flight. Soon, the skies over Heron Island are filled with the rushing shapes of wedge-tailed shearwaters on their return from the day's foraging far out at sea.

As soon as the first shearwaters have landed, crashing in untidy piles in the approximate location of their nesting burrows, a haunting chorus of their courtship song begins. The call is a long 'whooo-aah', the first syllable descending, the second rising in a long drawn out sigh which is followed by a coarse rasping as the singer rapidly inhales. There can be no sound on earth that is more enchanting.

Only at night and by torchlight can the unusual activities of the shearwaters be observed. Birds that have formed breeding pairs sit facing each other, rattling their bills and preening their partner's feathers. If another bird intrudes on this intimate mutual grooming, it is met by a hysterical, frenzied wail.

The shearwaters' engaging personalities are never more clearly portrayed than when they move about on land. Their aerodynamic flying shape has necessitated feet that are set well back down their long sleek bodies. Thrusting their heads forward to gain enough impetus for raising their bodies off the ground, the birds stagger forward with necks craning and webbed feet pattering with a rhythmic slap. Each waddling advancement lasts only a few yards before the shearwaters collapse on their haunches again.

The webbed feet are designed for use at sea where the shearwaters paddle across the surface chasing squid and small fish, but on land they also make useful digging implements. A breeding burrow may reach 2m (6ft) in length and while one shearwater busily excavates the tunnel with backward scoops of its feet, its partner usually waits patiently at the entrance, unperturbed by the rhythmic showers of sand descending over its body. When the burrow is complete, both adults often go to sea for a week or more in order to fish and build up their energy reserves. Following their return a single white egg is laid at the end of the burrow and the parents share the incubation. The chick hatches nearly two months later and as it grows in size and confidence it ventures to the burrow entrance where it crouches in a fluffy ball of grey down to wait for its nightly feed. Wedge-

A pair of wedge-tailed shearwaters reinforce their breeding bond by intimately preening each other's neck plumage and sporadically breaking into a wailing courtship song.

Portrait of a wedge-tailed shearwater. Crouching next to their breeding burrows and wailing their courtship song throughout the night, these beautiful birds seem oblivious of even the most curious of human observers – allowing detailed close-up sketches to be made.

tailed shearwaters nest in burrows on islands throughout the Indo-Pacific, while the smaller Audubon's shearwaters are common in the Caribbean, but more scattered in the Indian and Pacific Oceans.

The arrival of the breeding population of wedge-tailed shearwaters at the Capricorn Group is one of the major spectacles of the year. The entire colony of several thousand birds return to their nest sites on Heron Island over two or three days at an identical date in October each year. Over 750,000 individuals nest on nearby North West Island.

It is the daily pre-dawn departure of the shearwater colony that implants the most lasting memory. Over the years, shearwaters have created sandy runways, bare of any vegetation, extending from their burrows out into the foredunes behind the beach. As the time for take-off approaches, hundreds of the birds file out of their tunnelled homes and line up in single file at the start of their respective runways. The whoops and yelps of their chorus reach a crescendo as the first shearwaters manoeuvre into position. From the vantage of the beach, the sounds of

rapidly slapping webbed feet on well-worn sand grow louder as the leading birds accelerate towards the launching ramp of the sand dune's crest. A hop, skip and jump and the shearwaters are aloft. The transition from clumsy waddling land-birds to birds designed for aerial soaring is spectacular. Soon, shearwaters are leaping from the island at several points, but by the time the first hint of sunrise appears in the east, most, if not all, have vanished.

VISITORS FROM THE NORTH

An hour before dawn, shearwaters launch themselves from the crests of sand dunes. Once airborne they will feed at sea, returning to their nesting islands after sunset.

■

The eggs of the lesser golden plover are perfectly camouflaged amongst the grasses and mosses of the Arctic tundra in northern Siberia and Alaska. Each buff-coloured shell is decorated with dark spots and blotches, rendering a clutch virtually invisible to a potential predator such as a skua. During the nesting season, in June and July, the adult plovers are resplendent in their breeding plumage with black breast and face contrasting with upperparts of mottled brown and gold. When the chicks hatch, they soon begin scurrying around their parents searching for food, and after only a month they become independent young plovers. Having raised their offspring, the adults begin to show signs of restlessness. The Arctic winter is rapidly approaching, and food on the tundra is becoming scarce. Both of these environmental factors trigger an inborn response within each bird, urging it to move south, to migrate.

Along with numerous other tundra-breeding waders, including curlews, whimbrels, sanderlings, stints, tattlers, sandpipers, godwits, turnstones and other species of plover, the

A lesser golden plover, possessing some remnant black bands from its breeding plumage, takes advantage of low tide coinciding with midday to take a cooling wash in a beach rock pool on a Pacific coral island.

lesser golden plovers set off. The methods of navigation used by birds during their migrations are still something of a mystery. A variety of mechanisms are probably involved. By day, the birds can use the sun as a directive aid and they can also recognize familiar landmarks passing below – unless, of course, they are juveniles on their first migration. At night, the migrating birds may be able to navigate in relation to star patterns. In addition, factors such as ultrasound, smell and the alignment of the earth's magnetic field may play a role.

The waders follow specific paths or 'migration corridors' on their southward journey. A major corridor linking Eurasia with Africa passes through the Persian Gulf and the Red Sea. For many birds the coastal sandflats and creeks around these areas are their overwintering destinations, while others gather on the coral islands in the Persian Gulf or the Suakin and Dahlak archipelagoes in the Red Sea. Black-winged stilts, bar-tailed godwits, redshanks, curlews, dunlins, little stints, grey plovers and curlew sandpipers arrive each year to exploit the rich feeding grounds of the shallow coastal zones. More than a million birds overwinter in the Persian Gulf alone. They join a resident breeding population of Socotra cormorants, sooty gulls, red-billed tropicbirds and various terns. After a short period of resting and feeding, many of the migrant waders leave Arabia and complete their migration by flying south towards Africa and the Indian Ocean. The Seychelles are a popular destination.

Another migration corridor exists through south-east Asia, with flocks splitting east and west to overwinter on either the

A pair of Capricorn silvereyes huddle together under the branch of a *Casuarina* tree.

∎

A pair of Mongolian plovers fluff out their feathers for insulation against a cool evening breeze blowing across their roosting site on the beach.

PREVIOUS PAGE
Sunset in the South Pacific.

∎

Indian or Pacific Ocean coasts of Australia. Some of the waders that breed in Alaska may cross the Bering Strait to link up with this route, while others migrate straight into the central and southern regions of the Pacific.

The coral cays of the Great Barrier Reef are an ideal overwintering location: safe and isolated, yet set amongst intertidal reef flats with readily accessible sources of food. Over fourteen species of wader have been recorded in the Capricorn Group alone. During low tide, some fly to the exposed rubble drifts near the reef to feed on small marine creatures while others wander along the shorelines probing the sand or searching the beach rock for small worms and snails. As the tide ebbs, these foraging grounds begin to flood, and the waders with shorter legs, such as Mongolian plovers and terek sandpipers, are the first to return to the upper beach areas of the cay to roost. They are followed by larger species such as whimbrels and eastern curlews, and soon the beach is dotted with clusters of waders intermingling with crowds of terns and gulls.

ISLAND CASTAWAYS

When spring arrives in the northern hemisphere, the waders leave the coral islands and migrate back to their Arctic breeding areas. At the completion of their nesting season, various sea-birds also depart. Several months drifting above the vast tracts of oceans lie ahead of them before they return to breed again the following year. However, for many types of bird and other animals, the coral island is a permanent home where they must find all their food, shelter and breeding requirements in order to survive.

Despite the small size of a coral cay, a surprising number of land-birds become successful colonists. Resident species on Great Barrier Reef cays include silvereyes, kingfishers, rails and doves.

Buff-banded rails stomp through the thick leaf-litter of the *Pisonia* forest on outspread toes, tossing leaves aside to reveal hidden morsels of food such as cockroaches or centipedes. They often investigate the burrows of wedge-tailed shearwaters in their search for insects. The forest is a favoured hunting ground, but breeding pairs usually choose grassy clearings in the woodland or behind the sand dunes to raise their young in. The

Buff-banded rail.

■

nest is simply a flattened patch of grass and up to eight eggs are laid. The parents are extremely protective towards their clutch and will charge at intruders in a wing-lowered screaming rage. The tiny chicks are covered in black down and follow the adult birds wherever they go, rushing up to inspect each leaf or twig that the parents uncover as they forage.

Silvereyes feed on fruit and small insects as well as the nectar from large flowers which they lap up with their special brush-tipped tongues. Communal feeding flocks begin to break up into mating pairs at the onset of the breeding season. Males display to females by crouching on a nearby branch, fluttering their wings and calling with a soft cooing sigh. The dominant pairs claim territories in the most desirable locations. A fig tree often lies within their boundaries and will provide a convenient source of food for both the adults and their offspring. Strands of grass are woven into an intricate cup-shaped nest which is suspended by individual fibrous threads tied around a forked branch high up in a tree or within a dense shrub. Once the nest is lined with an insulating bedding of silk, torn from the webs of orb spiders, it is ready for its clutch of three to four pale blue eggs.

A flock of grey-tailed tattlers roost on the branches of a dead *Pisonia* tree. At low tide, they forage along the wet sands of the beach, walking rapidly with jerky head movements and occasionally pausing to extract worms from sand burrows. Grey-tailed tattlers breed in the mountainous regions of northern Siberia and overwinter in south-east Asia and the western South Pacific.

■

The sacred kingfisher excavates a hole in the trunk of a *Pisonia* tree or *Pandanus* palm in which to lay its eggs. Bar-shouldered doves also nest in *Pandanus* palms, but construct a platform of twigs in the fork of a branch.

On some of the Belize Barrier Reef cays, tiny cinnamon hummingbirds have colonized from Central America. Flitting between coconut palms and feeding on nectar from their long flowering spikes, the hummingbirds have established themselves as breeding residents. A miniscule dome-shaped nest with a depression in the top is constructed on a branch of the shoreline

An anolid lizard adopts a threatening head-raised posture from the domed surface of a fallen coconut that lies within its territory.

■

gombo-limbo trees. Other breeding birds include mangrove warblers and great-tailed grackles. The latter are glossy black crow-sized birds with strong bills and prominent wedge-shaped tails.

On the larger volcanic and continental islands, there is a greater range of habitats for land-birds to exploit. The high islands of the Caribbean, for example, support a rich mixture of cloud forests, rainforests, scrub woodland and coastal thicket which are inhabited by numerous land-birds such as doves, hummingbirds, bellbirds and parrots. High islands may also possess mountain valleys and caves that offer protection against severe weather, enabling the survival of species that would otherwise succumb to swamping waves and strong winds on a low-lying coral cay.

The ancestors of most Pacific land-birds have an Asiatic or Australian origin. Fruit pigeons, kingfishers, white-eyes, swiftlets, honey-eaters, megapodes, rails, flycatchers and warblers have gradually dispersed from the western fringe of the Pacific Ocean, fanning out through the island chains of Micronesia and Melanesia, and becoming scarcer in the eastern archipelagoes of Polynesia furthest from the mainland source.

In contrast to the diverse birdlife found on many coral islands, native species of land mammal are extremely scarce. The only family likely to be encountered are the fruit bats. Over two hundred species are found throughout the mainland tropics and a few, such as the Tongan flying fox, have managed to penetrate into the western fringes of the central Pacific. Fruit bats have very large eyes, enabling them to use normal vision instead of echolocation – the method used by the other major group of bats, the insect eaters. As their name implies, the fruit bats are vegetarian, leaving their tree or cave roosts at dusk to feed on ripe fruits in the forest. With long fox-like faces and strong jaws, they are capable of breaking open hard-shelled fruits to reach the soft flesh inside.

Lizards and reptiles are far more widespread on islands. Even on coral cays there are often populations of small geckos and skinks. Anolid lizards have colonized most of the Caribbean islands. The males possess a loose dewlap of skin which hangs from their throat and can be fanned out when displaying to a prospective mate. In some species, the dewlap is brightly coloured and acts as a bold advertisement, but on the island of Hispaniola, a small variety of anolid has evolved a far less conspicuous dewlap in order to avoid detection by predators. All male anolid lizards are strongly territorial and will rush up to a rival and aggressively bob their heads up and down.

Two larger species of lizard, the wish willy and scaly-tailed

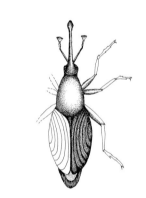

This large weevil was sketched as it scurried across the trunk of a coconut palm on Hunting Cay (Belize Barrier Reef) probing in cracks with its long proboscis in search of food.

■

146

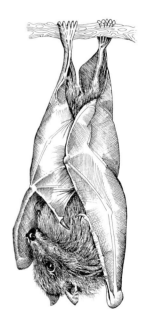

The courtship display of the bar-shouldered dove is an elaborate one. The male (*right*) begins by nuzzling the neck plumage of the female before turning and strutting a few paces away. After a short pause, he suddenly fans his tail and stretches his neck upwards. On this occasion, however, the female seems unimpressed.

∎

The sweet flesh of the Tongan flying fox (or fruit bat) is popular with islanders in many parts of the South Pacific. Some populations are becoming increasingly scarce as a result of over-hunting.

∎

iguana, inhabit Half Moon Cay at Lighthouse Reef, one of the atolls lying to the east of the Belize Barrier Reef, while Anegada iguanas are endemic to the Virgin Islands. Another large species of iguana is found only on the Yasawa Islands in Fiji where it was discovered as recently as 1978. This, the Fijian crested iguana, is something of an island enigma since its closest relatives are the iguanas of Caribbean islands. For it to have reached the western Pacific Ocean its ancestors must have rafted out of the Caribbean Sea on pieces of floating vegetation when the Panama Isthmus was covered by sea some seven million years ago.

Large sand goannas are common on the reef-fringed continental islands near the Queensland coast of Australia, but these were probably established before the islands became separated from the mainland. Several other species of monitor lizard, stranded on islands in a similar manner, are found throughout the Indonesian Archipelago, the largest being the 3m (9ft) long Komodo dragon. Monitor lizards, together with a few species of snake such as the Pacific boa and Palau tree snake, are also found on the larger islands of Micronesia.

EVOLUTION IN ISOLATION

Only relatively few species of plants and land animals are destined to colonize a remote island. The more isolated the island is, the less likely it is to receive a variety of colonists. Those that are successful in making landfall become detached from their parent populations which may be many thousands of miles away on the nearest continent. The island castaways are effectively severed from the rest of their species. No longer are they influenced by inhibiting aspects of a mainland lifestyle. Indeed, an island presents the successful colonists with a world of opportunities, and the powerful shaping force of evolution enables these to be fulfilled.

No amphibians, reptiles, mammals or conifers have ever reached Hawaii by natural means of dispersal. They are the most isolated group of islands in the world. Only a few land-birds and various plants and insects have managed to cross the wide expanses of the Pacific Ocean to reach them. Around twenty million years ago, a group of small finch-like birds related to the tanagers arrived on Hawaii having flown from North America. They may have been blown out to sea from their native mainland habitat or may have simply lost their way during a migration and, quite by chance, discovered the islands. The exact circumstances of their dispersal will never be known, but there is living proof of the subsequent success of their colonization. Over forty new species of bird are known to have evolved from the original ancestral flock. How could this have happened?

It is highly likely that Hawaii had very few, if any, species of small land-bird when the colonists from North America arrived. All the comparable niches that such birds occupy on the mainland were vacant on Hawaii. A single species of bird, however, could not occupy all the niches since each one demanded a certain set of adaptations before it could be exploited. To begin with, therefore, the ancestral birds were restricted to a lifestyle similar to the one they had led in North America. They fed on seeds and began to breed.

It was only after many generations that the first changes started to take place. In small populations, in-breeding is unavoidable, and gradually gives rise to mutations in the offspring. In mature, well-established communities, individuals with these alterations may be unable to survive, but on an island which offers a variety of unexploited niches, they stand a far greater chance.

On Hawaii, those birds that were born with slightly longer and more slender bills than their predecessors found they could feed more effectively on small insects. Not only did this new foraging method avoid competition with the original seed-eating

The Hawaiian honeycreepers demonstrate a remarkable variation in the shapes and sizes of their bills. Each is well suited for a particular feeding strategy. *From top to bottom:* the Laysan finch is a specialist breaker of Laysan albatross eggs and may also feed on seeds; the palila crushes open the pods of the mamane trees while the Maui parrotbill uses its robust bill to crack open twigs in search of burrowing beetle larvae. The anianiau has a much finer bill for picking insects off leaves and stems or occasionally for sipping nectar from a flower. The i'iwi specializes in the nectar from the flowers of the ohia and mamane trees, and the akiapolaau hunts for insects under the bark of trees by hammering with its shorter lower mandible and extracting its prey with its longer, curved upper one. The akialoa uses its fine bill to probe the cracks in bark for insects, but this honeycreeper is also well adapted for reaching the nectar in obeliads.

forms, but it allowed a new niche to be exploited. Gradually, other feeding strategies evolved and over thousands of years the ancestral colonizing stock radiated into many variations. Subtle differences that helped a bird to fit into its new habitat were favoured by evolution and became selected as dominant features in the bird's genetic make-up. Eventually, the differences became so pronounced that entirely new species arose. They are Hawaii's own special family of birds – the honeycreepers.

The present day diversity of the honeycreepers is quite extraordinary. The i'iwi has a long, slender curving bill which fits perfectly into the flowers of the ohi'a tree from which it sips nectar. Other species have large robust bills for crushing seeds or narrow forcep-like bills for extracting insect larvae from their burrows in wood. The Laysan finch is perhaps the most unusual of all the honeycreepers for it has evolved a robust beak, not for grinding seeds, but for breaking into the eggs of the Laysan albatross. Once the shell has been fractured, the carnivorous little bird feeds on the contents. Laysan finches are also reputed to have taken on the role of vampire bats, by lapping blood from wounds on the adult sea-birds.

Adaptive radiation is the term used to describe the branching evolutionary history of an ancestral stock of plants or animals into a wide range of new species. The honeycreepers are one of the most well-known examples, but similar evolutionary trends have resulted in unique forms of *Lobelia* plants, *Drosophila* flies and *Achatinella* snails on Hawaii and a complete family of finches in the Galapagos Islands.

When plants and animals make landfall on a remote island they become isolated, and over many generations they often evolve into unique species endemic to a particular island.

Evolution has affected other island species in different ways. For example, tortoises on Aldabra and the Galapagos Islands have become giants, and the longhorn beetles of Fiji are some of the largest insects in the world. There are certainly advantages in possessing a greater body size. Males can compete more effectively for mates, while females can lay more eggs. Smaller individuals, on the other hand, require less food and are able to hide from predators. However, since large carnivores cannot be sustained on an island, it appears that there is no benefit to be gained by remaining small and inconspicuous. Indeed, the giant tortoise has become enlarged in such a manner that it is now incapable of withdrawing its vulnerable neck and head inside its shell. If a tortoise inhabiting the plains of East Africa evolved along this path it would rapidly be exterminated by hunters such as hyaenas. An additional evolutionary incentive for becoming an island giant is that it provides the tortoise with access to a wider range of food sources. With its head mounted on a long neck the tortoise can browse on the leaves of small bushes as well as reaching down to pluck at ground vegetation.

Not only is the Rarotongan *Fitchia* tree unique, but it is also the only habitat for a tiny species of weevil, which feeds on the leaves. In addition, an endemic starling sips nectar from the tree's flowers providing a pollination service. An interdependent community has evolved around one variety of tree growing on one island in the middle of the Pacific Ocean. If this delicate web of life was damaged by human activity it would be impossible to recreate.

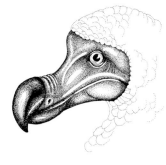

The dodo is only one of dozens, perhaps hundreds, of island bird species that have become extinct since man first began colonizing the world's remote islands. Hunting, habitat destruction and the introduction of harmful species such as rats have all played a role.

On islands where food is scarce, or during periods of drought, some have even been known to feed on the carcasses of dead tortoises.

Most birds rely on flight to escape predators, expending a great deal of energy operating large flight muscles. On islands which are predator-free, it is an expense some birds have found unnecessary and they have become flightless. Scurrying in between the slow-moving giant tortoises on Aldabra are white-throated rails which can no longer fly. Many of the Pacific islands have, at some time, supported their own endemic species of flightless rail although fewer species remain today. On New Caledonia, a relative of the cranes, known as the kagu, has also progressed along the evolutionary path to flightlessness, as have the cormorants of the Galapagos Islands.

The absence of predators is probably not the only explanation for why a flying animal should gradually evolve into a flightless one. On Hawaii there are lacewings which have either lost their wings altogether or have developed heavy non-functional ones. Lacewings are small insects and there are

Hidden within the dense natural forests of the Pacific's high islands are endemic populations of land-bird including fruit doves, starlings and flycatchers.

ABOVE LEFT
A white-breasted waterhen (of the rail family) forages along the water's edge on a coral cay in the Maldives, passing the volcano-shaped mound of sand excavated from a ghost crab burrow.

■

certainly creatures on Hawaii capable of hunting them. However, by retaining the ability of flight to help escape predation they would increase the chances of being accidentally blown out to sea.

The white-throated rails are the only remaining flightless birds in the Indian Ocean. In the recent past, however, Mauritius was home to the dodo, a pigeon (or, according to some biologists, a relative of the rails) which had not only lost the power of flight, but had become a giant as well. So used to a world without any predators, the dodos were merely curious of the first humans who arrived at Mauritius. Sadly, the dodo and the related solitaires of nearby Reunion and Rodriguez Islands were rapidly battered into extinction. Today, the image of the dodo symbolizes the irreparable damage that humans can wreak amongst island plant and animal communities. All ecosystems develop a natural balance which is susceptible to the impact of human disturbance, but islands are particularly vulnerable, since the loss of a population often means the extinction of an entire endemic species.

FOOTPRINTS IN PARADISE

THE ARRIVAL OF MAN

OPPOSITE
Small outrigger canoes, known as *vaa*, are used by the Polynesian islanders for fishing in the sheltered reef-enclosed waters of the lagoon. To reach the remote Pacific islands in the first place, they used much larger canoes equipped with two hulls and a sail.

■

Bathed in isolation by their surrounding coral seas, the world's tropical islands support well-adapted communities of plants and animals. Only those species which possess suitable methods of dispersal were able to make landfall and their success as colonists depended on whether they could fit into the whole ecological framework of the existing ecosystem. Some were so successful that, over millions of years, they evolved into a whole range of new island species that could take advantage of unclaimed niches. Everything worked together to create a natural balance. But then the islands received a new arrival. This creature was totally different to any other island species. It was a large mammal; the type of animal that small island worlds would usually be unable to support through lack of space and natural resources. However, such restrictions did not greatly affect this species. Its name was *Homo sapiens*, the human being, and ever since small groups of humans wandered north out of the cradle of their evolution in Africa, they learned how to cope with each new landscape they encountered by using their large brains to solve problems.

Around fifty thousand years ago, the human break-out from Africa was well under way. Hunter-gatherers had become established across much of Europe and Asia. At this time the world was gripped in an ice age and the sea level was much lower than it is today, since huge volumes of water had become trapped in the polar ice caps. As the oceans shrank, shallow seas were transformed into plains of dry land. The Andaman Islands, Indonesia and Borneo were joined to the Asian mainland by the exposed Sunda Shelf, while to the south-east, New Guinea and Australia had also merged to form a single land mass. These two regions were separated by an oval sea which still occupied the Banda Basin. A chain of small islands stretched across the sea's

The European discoverer of Aitutaki Atoll in the Cook Islands was Captain William Bligh aboard the *Bounty* on 11 April 1789; seventeen days before the mutiny. In 1835, Charles Darwin visited the atoll and four years later the first missionary from Europe was established. During the 1850s, Aitutaki was a popular stop-over for whalers. More recently, flying boats used to refuel there during the days of the Pacific Coral Route.

Lower sea levels some 50,000 years ago gave rise to extended regions of dry land across much of south-east Asia, shortening the sea crossings human beings would have to have made in order to reach Australia and eventually the Pacific Ocean via the Bismarck Archipelago. This map reconstructs a possible outline of the land masses during the period of extreme low sea level (vertical green lines) and also shows the present-day distribution of land (solid green) and two of the likely routes of human migration (red arrows).

■

southern limit in a path of stepping stones from Bali to Timor, and reached to within 100km (62 miles) of northern Australia. The island of Sulawesi remained isolated, but only a very narrow channel separated it from the expanded shoreline of Borneo. From the eastern coast of Sulawesi, the Moluccas Islands branched out towards New Guinea.

The wandering humans were able to walk as far as Java and Borneo. Some settled in the forests that covered the mountainous interiors, while others gathered in communities along the coast. The shoreline dwellers knew how to harvest the resources of estuaries and offshore waters, and this must have involved a basic knowledge of fishing and boat building. At least forty thousand years ago some of them crossed to Australia and New Guinea, paddling simple rafts between the island chains that provided such an ideal link between the two areas of mainland. The first Australian Aborigines settled the exposed continental shelf of Queensland long before the present day Great Barrier Reef began forming. Archaeologists believe they will one day discover limestone caves now flooded, but once inhabited by Aborigines during this period of low sea level. As the climate gradually warmed, causing the ice to melt and the oceans to swell, the Aborigines withdrew towards mainland Australia.

Around ten thousand years ago, New Guinea began to be separated from Australia and seas also began to encroach across the Sunda Shelf, fragmenting Indonesia into its former island chain and isolating Borneo and the Philippines. Another land-bridge across the Bering Strait was also flooded, but not before humans had crossed from Asia to America. In fact, man probably entered the Americas as early as forty-five thousand years ago and rapidly spread southwards. Humans now occupied all the major continents, but no race had yet ventured into the vast tracts of the oceans in search of new land.

The first people to develop the necessary skills for purposeful sea crossings probably originated in southern China. They were the Mongoloids (a major ethnic division which now includes the Eskimos, American Indians, Mongolians, Chinese and Malayans) and at least ten thousand years ago they crossed the Malay Peninsula to reach the Indonesian archipelago. The Mongoloids were more advanced than the hunter-gatherers who still lived in the forests or by the coast. They knew how to cultivate crops such as taro and yam and they had also domesticated the Asiatic wildfowl and forest pig. Furthermore, they were skilled fishermen who fashioned harpoons and hooks from pieces of bone and flint, and constructed nets from interwoven fibres. The Mongoloids also knew how to design and build ocean-going canoes. Four to five thousand years ago their descendants had colonized islands as far east as the Bismarck Archipelago and the Solomon Group, and from there man ventured north and east to settle Micronesia and the rest of Melanesia. The remains of a village at Bikini Atoll in the Marshall Islands have been dated to 1960BC, making it the site of one of the earliest human settlements yet discovered in Micronesia. The Marshallese constructed stick charts to use as navigational aids when travelling between the low-lying coral cays of the atolls. Several flat strips of wood were tied together in designs which imitated the pattern of waves, and shells were attached to denote the position of islands.

Around three thousand years ago, on the isolated islands of Fiji, Samoa and Tonga, a distinct race of humans emerged who possessed an even greater mastery of the ocean. These were the Polynesians, and in their huge twin-hulled *pahi* canoes which measured 33m (100ft) in length and carried a single triangular

Following the extinction of the dodo, a species of tree endemic to Mauritius went into decline. The dodo used to provide an important dispersal service for the seeds of the *Calvaria major* tree by eating its fruit.

Detailed drawing of an adult bridled tern. This unfortunate individual was found dead in the sand dune region of Heron Island where it may well have collapsed from exhaustion after being blown from its nesting island during a long period of stormy weather.

■

CORAL REEFS & ISLANDS

On many of the less westernized islands of the Pacific, the Polynesians still make traditional use of a variety of special plants. The Polynesian hibiscus, which the islanders introduced themselves, produces exotic red flowers, the petals of which are crushed to make a herbal medicine. The larger blooms of the tree hibiscus are used to treat cuts, while its bark can be torn into strips for hula skirts and rope. The nut of the Polynesian chestnut is boiled with coconut juice to make a popular traditional dish, and the fruit of the *Melastoma* shrub is also eaten. Frangipani flowers and fragrant leaves of the *Alyxia* shrub are woven into decorative headbands or long necklace-like *leis* to be worn round the neck. A variety of ginger is used for shampoo and the Kava Maori plant was traditionally used in the production of a relaxing narcotic drink, until the European missionaries banned its cultivation.

sail, they set out to colonize the rest of the Pacific Ocean. By the year AD750 they had succeeded. Using their intimate knowledge of the sea, the Polynesians had established themselves as the most widely-spread people on earth. Their sea-lore, acquired through experience and tradition, involved a wide range of navigational techniques. They memorized 'star paths' which helped them to navigate by night, and during the day they studied distant clouds which changed colour as they passed over land. They could interpret patterns of swells and trails of drifting vegetation and may even have followed the routes of migratory wading birds such as the wandering tattler and golden plover as they journeyed from the Arctic tundra to their wintering grounds on islands across the Pacific.

The Polynesians relied heavily on the sea for food during their long voyages, catching fish, turtles, sea-birds, and dolphins. The sea alone, however, could not sustain them indefinitely. They realized the value of fruits and vegetables, and these they carried with them as seeds and cuttings, along with their chickens, pigs and dogs. All of these items could be eaten, providing the voyagers with an alternative to their predominantly seafood diet, but this was not the only reason they loaded them on board their canoes at the start of a new sea journey. Small islands, in their natural state, are poorly equipped to support humans. They have few, if any, edible plants and animals. Therefore, when the Polynesians made landfall, they arrived with their own life-support systems and, armed with a knowledge of farming, they immediately began to create their own environment. This involved slashing and burning the natural lowland forests to make way for their crops, which included yams, taro, coconuts, banana, breadfruit, arrowroot and gourd. Taro was their staple food since both its leaf and root could be eaten. The coconut, on the other hand, was one of the most useful. Its trunk could be used for building houses and boats, the leaves for constructing roofs and bed matting, the roots for medicines and dyes, and fibrous strands could be woven together to make cord.

Many of the coastal forests on the high volcanic islands of the Pacific were devastated. Sea-birds that had nested in the trees and shrubs along the shoreline fled to other islands to seek refuge, as did the turtles which had used the beaches for egg laying. Many species of indigenous land-bird became extinct in the wake of the Polynesian arrival. It has been estimated that on Hawaii alone nearly forty species were eradicated, including an ibis and a flightless goose. Other birds may have escaped into the mountainous interior of the islands where man rarely went since it was too difficult to cultivate crops on the steep-sided valleys. The people spent most of their time on the low coastal plains,

156

The Polynesians introduced taro to many Pacific islands where it is still grown as a source of carbohydrate-rich food. Terraced plots fed by mountain streams provide the swampy conditions necessary for cultivating the crop.

■

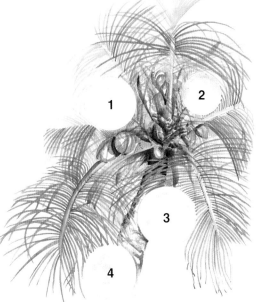

The coconut palm has an incredible range of human uses.

1. Coconut and fruit: food and drink for journeys and in villages, storage containers, means of transporting palm to other islands.

2. Fibre: cord and rope, fishing nets.

3. Fronds: bed matting, roof thatching, clothing, baskets, canoe decking.

4. Trunk: housing material, boat building, crafts, tools.

■

but their domesticated animals roamed freely. Dogs chased ground-nesting birds such as rails, while pigs began to wreak havoc amongst the native plant life, either by trampling it or consuming it in vast quantities. Evolution had endowed the plants with few, if any, defences (such as thorns or chemicals) with which to combat the alien herbivores – before man arrived, there was no requirement for them.

The low sandy islands on coral atolls were less hospitable to the Polynesians for they often had little surface-water and were particularly susceptible to storm-driven winds and waves. They were probably visited for short periods at certain times of the year when turtle and sea-bird eggs could be harvested. Some of the coral cays supported nesting colonies of the red-tailed tropicbird, an important source of ornamental feathers. The Cook Islanders were renowned for their spectacular head-dresses, made from the birds' long streaming tail feathers, which they collected at Aitutaki and Takutea. On the high islands of Hawaii, the Polynesian chiefs donned exotic cloaks made from the feathers of hundreds of tiny honeycreepers, including the scarlet-coloured i'iwi.

By the time the Polynesians had settled the Pacific Ocean, other races of humans had discovered many of the coral islands in the Indian Ocean and Caribbean Sea. The coral atolls of the

Maldives, for example, were probably inhabited as early as 500BC by voyagers from Sri Lanka and India. The early Maldivians depended largely on the sea for food, but the south-west monsoons brought enough rain to support crops such as breadfruit and yam. As the population increased, the coconut palm, which was to play such an essential role in the lives of the islanders, was introduced throughout the chain of atolls, replacing the indigenous *Pisonia* forests and eradicating many sea-bird colonies.

On some Belize Barrier Reef cays in the Caribbean, archaeologists have discovered the remains of Maya Indian fishing settlements which date back to 300BC. Canoeing on the sheltered reef waters, the Maya collected fish, turtle eggs, manatees, sea-birds and conch. While some of this produce was eaten, a large proportion was exchanged for crops at inland settlements.

As each island culture became established in different parts of the world, it developed the need to trade. At first, all trade was conducted within island groups and forms of currency were developed which could be used to denote the value of goods. Shells collected from the reefs and beaches were a popular choice. Today, oyster-shell necklaces are still used in the Solomon Islands to purchase wives. It was in the Maldive and Laccadive Islands, however, that a certain type of shell was

Fish has always been the main source of protein for the inhabitants of the Maldivian Archipelago. Fishermen in traditional sailing *dhonis* ply the reef waters in search of skipjack.

ABOVE LEFT
Humpback whales used to be hunted in the waters of the Great Barrier Reef, but numbers had declined so severely by the 1960s that whaling operations had to be closed down. Humpbacks are now listed as an endangered species by CITES and receive international protection. Research in Queensland and Hawaii suggests a slow, but positive, recovery of the Pacific populations.

collected in enormous quantities for use as a currency. Cowries were in such demand by the Arabians for their trade with the Far East, that the Maldives became known as the Money Isles. The Maldivians had probably been trading with Arabia, India and China for several centuries before a full and reliable account, in AD1343, revealed details of the produce involved. In addition to the cowries, other trade goods included dried fish, coconuts, turtle shells and ambergris – a musky wax from the intestines of sperm whales which was used in the production of perfumes.

During the late 1400s and early 1500s, explorers from Europe began to discover routes into the Pacific and Indian Oceans as well as the Caribbean Sea. In the wake of Magellan, Da Gama and Columbus, came a host of seafarers intent on exploiting the riches of the exotic new lands. In the mid 1770s, trade ships began visiting the Seychelles where they were supplied with hardwood from the native forests, as well as live giant tortoises which could provide a source of fresh meat during the ongoing voyage.

The Pacific islands are devoid of gold or spices and, to begin with, they were used as stop-overs where stores could be replenished before sailing on to the Moluccas 'spice' islands and the wealthy markets of Asia. It was not long, however, before the commercial potential of the islands was realized. In the 1800s,

Tied to a nearby tree, a pig ploughs the ground with its snout, in search of food. On Hawaii, introduced domestic pigs which have escaped into the wild are wreaking irreparable damage to fragile endemic plant species.

■

sandalwood trees were being torn from the slopes of Hawaii, New Caledonia and Fiji to supply Chinese markets with aromatic wood for use as joss-sticks, incense and perfumes.

At the same time, whaling ships set out into the Pacific. As they quartered the ocean searching for sperm whales, they charted many coral atolls and islands and by the time the American and British whaling boom of the 1840s was over there was hardly a speck of land left undiscovered. After this first significant contact with foreigners, the Pacific islanders were left decimated by smallpox, measles, whooping cough and venereal disease; ailments to which they had no natural resistance.

A cultural impact was soon to follow, as missionaries spread throughout the archipelagoes. Traditional ways of life were swept away and spiritual links with nature were shattered. Colonial rule descended over many parts of the Pacific Ocean, allowing the resources of the coral reefs and islands to be exploited in a controlled and effective manner.

Throughout the tropics, large areas of natural island forest were converted to coconut plantations for supplying the world trade in coconut oil and copra. Other areas were planted with sugar cane, coffee, pineapple, cotton and rubber, and the islanders were enslaved to work in the agricultural estates. Cattle and goat herds were introduced and immediately began trampling the nesting burrows of petrels and shearwaters and browsing on vulnerable island plant life. Other human introductions, such as ship rats and domestic cats, preyed on ground-nesting and flightless birds, often with fatal consequences for entire species. To decorate the paradise he had found, man also established numerous exotic species of ornamental plant which have since out-competed native ones.

Many islands which had once been major sea-bird rookeries were plundered for their soil. Guano deposits, created over thousands of years by the build-up of phosphate-rich bird excrement, are still of enormous value as a fertilizer. On the small island of Nauru in Micronesia, over one hundred million tonnes have been extracted since mining began in the early 1900s. Today, as a result of guano mining, the Nauruans earn the highest per-capita incomes in the world, but their island has been irreparably scarred.

Coral reefs also began to provide the raw materials for various industries. Sea cucumbers were harvested in huge quantities during the 1800s, and exported from the tropical Indo-Pacific as dried and smoked *beche-de-mer*. In the Far East, the shrivelled, black bodies of the sea cucumbers are still regarded as a delicacy. Pearl oysters, green snails and trochus shells also began to be harvested from the reef waters and they continue to

Oil and copra are processed from coconuts. When the value of these products was realized, the natural forests of coral islands throughout the world began to be cleared to make way for coconut palm plantations.

■

The introduced common mynah bird is well adapted to urban environments and has reached high densities in the developed coastal regions of many Pacific Islands.

supply a trade in jewellery and fashion accessories made from mother-of-pearl. Turtle canneries were established at nesting sites, such as Heron Island on the Great Barrier Reef, to exploit the annual influx of egg-laying females for the production of turtle soup.

Elsewhere, sea cow, monk seal and crocodile populations started to slide towards extinction under the relentless persecution of hunters armed with guns. On some islands, the well-aimed blows of a club or rifle butt were sufficient to consign unwary and defenceless birds like the dodo to extinction.

Without doubt, nuclear testing must rank as the single most devastating form of environmental impact to have been unleashed on coral islands and reefs. Only in 1992 did France (the last nation to test nuclear weapons in the Pacific Ocean) declare its intention to end its nuclear programme in French Polynesia.

The 'peaceful' waters of the ocean that the Portuguese navigator Ferdinand Magellan had been inspired to name 'the Pacific' in 1519, are now restless in the turbulent wake of more than 450 years of subsequent human use. The coral reefs and islands of this great ocean, together with those of the Indian and

161

Ever since humans began voyaging across the oceans, they have solved the problems of dispersal for a wide variety of plants and animals that would otherwise have had great difficulty in reaching islands. Inconspicuous insects, plant seeds, geckos and lizards have found suitable niches on islands after arriving as stowaways aboard Polynesian canoes, Arabian *dhows*, Spanish galleons and American tallships. Today, cruise ships and jet-powered airliners ensure the continued distribution of accidental introductions.

Many of these invaders have settled on islands at the considerable expense of existing native species. In the Seychelles, for example, one of the main threats to the survival of the indigenous coco-de-mer palm is competition from more robust introduced plants. Other intruders have caused havoc amongst island bird communities. An island inhabited by ground-nesting sea-birds and flightless rails is a paradise for rats. These small but effective carnivores have been observed launching mass attacks on the nesting colonies of terns; leaping at the throats of the adults and plundering their nests for eggs and chicks. Sea-birds are able to relocate their breeding

sites, but endemic populations of flightless rail are less fortunate. Rats have caused the extinction of several species of tropical Pacific rail, and many other indigenous land-birds, such as the Fijian long-legged warbler, face a similar fate.

The black ship rat and Norwegian brown rat are the two most notorious bird killers, and have been inadvertently carried to islands since Europeans first set sail on their 'voyages of discovery' nearly five hundred years ago. Another species, known as the Polynesian rat, was once believed to pose far less of a threat to island birdlife, but recently a population on Henderson Island was found to be gorging itself on Murphy's petrel chicks to the point of destroying the nesting colony altogether.

In an attempt to control an unwanted species such as a rat, other predators have been *deliberately* introduced to some islands. The East African barn owl, for example, was released in the Seychelles (in sufficient numbers to ensure its breeding success) with the intention of establishing a rat-eating bird on the islands. Unfortunately, the barn owls preferred to prey on white terns and became a pest themselves. With a similar lack of forethought, the

mongoose has been introduced to many Caribbean islands to control rats. The fact that the mongoose hunts by day and would, therefore, rarely encounter the nocturnal rat was apparently overlooked and now they both prey on native birds such as the endangered white-breasted thrasher. In 1873, the Indian mongoose was released on Fiji to prey on rats, but instead eight species of land-bird were eaten into extinction.

A mass slaughter of rare endemic birds is currently taking place on the Micronesian island of Guam, but the animal responsible is not a rat or a mongoose, but a snake. The brown tree snake probably arrived on Guam as an accidental introduction from ships soon after the

Second World War. With no natural predators or other biological controls to keep it in balance, the population has exploded with devastating consequences for the island's land-birds – the principal diet of the snake. Already nine out of the twelve endemic species found on Guam have been wiped out. The Micronesian kingfisher and Guam rail survive only in captive breeding programmes in zoos. There are now fears that the brown tree snake may spread to other islands in the Pacific Ocean and ravage their bird communities. Already, snakes have been found in aircraft flying from Guam to Hawaii.

By adapting to an existence closely associated with humans, the black and brown rats have become two of the most widespread and successful mammals, spreading across most of the planet's surface as stowaways aboard ships. Their acute hearing and eyesight, keen sense of smell and sensitive vibrissae (or groups of long hairs on the head) help these rodents to be efficient scavengers in human settlements as well as effective hunters in the wild.

The queen conch is native to the Caribbean and its meat has long been of importance to commercial fisheries in countries such as Belize. Nearly 550 000kg (1.2 million lb) were exported by the fishery in 1972 and the conch has since gone into serious decline. Huge drifts of discarded shells piled onto beaches are a reflection of the overfishing.

■

Atlantic Oceans, have reeled from the impact of the human invasion. Today, there are no islands awaiting discovery; man has laid claim to the most remote archipelagoes and has mapped each one from space. Pristine coral reefs and islands, however, still exist in many parts of the world, but these fragments of untainted paradise are becoming increasingly rare. Growing threats to their survival, both on a local and global scale, are the sad realities of a modern world dominated by vast numbers of humans over-exploiting its natural resources.

HUMAN IMPACT

Ever since man settled on the coastlines of tropical seas, he has harvested the marine life from nearby coral reefs for food. Traditional methods of fishing, using basic equipment, still thrive in many parts of the world and provide an important protein component in the diet of many coastal subsistence communities. Inevitably, however, they have been largely replaced by more advanced and efficient techniques which can supply food not only to growing local populations, but also to a profitable export trade.

Unfortunately, these modern fishing methods are more likely to adversely affect coral reef ecosystems, either directly or indirectly. The use of explosives, for example, causes considerable structural damage to the reef framework itself. Damaging the ecosystem in this manner makes it extremely unlikely that it will ever yield a sustainable source of fish again. After an initial large dynamited harvest of fish, a reef may take several decades to recover to its former diversity – if revival is possible at all. Fishing using explosives is especially prevalent in south-east Asia, where other reef-damaging techniques such as poisoning and reef trawling also take place.

Selective overfishing of certain species can upset the natural food-web of the reef. Large groupers often occupy resident territories, making them easy targets for snorkellers or divers equipped with spearguns. As these natural predators become depleted, their prey starts to flourish, reaching high densities and displacing other species which are no longer able to compete with them for food and living space. Similarly, overfishing of herbivorous species allows algae to spread unchecked across the reef and also reduces the amount of food available to predators. Unexploited reefs, that are allowed to retain their naturally balanced populations of fish, are important 'pools' from which impoverished reefs can recruit the drifting larval stages of overfished species. Research in Florida, however, suggests that once the balance is disrupted it is not easily restored.

Commercial and recreational fishing are significant

A harvest of Maldivian beche-de-mer (gutted and smoked sea cucumbers) ready for export to restaurants in the Far East.

■

At the current rate of coral mining, the entire North Male Atoll could be bare by the year 2014.

■

industries in many reef areas, generating local employment and considerable revenues. Different regions support a wide variety of fisheries. On the Great Barrier Reef, prawn trawling is the most important, whereas tuna comprises the dominant catch around the Maldives and across much of the South Pacific. To increase efficiency, some fleets trail vast ocean-stripping drift-nets which severely deplete fish stocks and ensnare and drown many non-target species such as turtles, dolphins and sea-birds. In the Caribbean, the queen conch and spiny lobster populations have been decimated by excessive and unregulated fishing. The Caribbean monk seal is almost certainly extinct as a result of over-exploitation and the endangered manatee (the meat of which is still for sale in some markets) is heading towards a similar fate.

As major stocks of important commercial species such as the anchovies off Peru, the pilchards off Namibia and the salmon, tuna and squid in the Pacific continue to dwindle, fishing industries may have to rely more heavily on the world's coral reefs, to meet the demands of a growing human population. This would pose serious threats not only to the balance and diversity of reef ecosystems, but also to the breeding success of sea-bird colonies on coral islands. When sand eel numbers plummeted as a result of overfishing in the North Sea, local nesting populations of Arctic terns and kittiwakes suffered several years of breeding failure. Adult birds were unable to find enough sand eels to feed their hatchlings. The situation improved only after the population of sand eels increased following a ban on their collection; a similar scenario could be envisaged with sea-birds which breed in the tropics.

An escalating human population will also precipitate a demand for more agriculture and industry, both of which already threaten coral reef and island ecosystems. The problems fall into two main categories: direct structural damage and indirect pollution.

Coral and sand are mined from reefs throughout the Indo-Pacific and Caribbean for use as lime and for road and building materials. Once the living veneer of corals is scraped from the reef the exposed framework is blasted apart, allowing shattered boulders of limestone to be extracted. Island habitats are devastated by phosphate mining operations as well as copra plantations and various forms of fruit and vegetable cultivation.

Mangrove forests surrounding islands or growing along mainland reef-fringed coasts are cleared to make way for more farmland. Removal of the complex meshwork of mangrove roots immediately destabilizes the swamp silts and muds, and exposes the shoreline to erosion. The sediment is then washed out to sea,

along with the soil run-off caused by rainforest clearance further inland, and the herbicides, pesticides, fertilizers, sewage and industrial waste from other human activities. Hazy clouds of sediment and chemicals engulf nearby reefs, subjecting the corals to various forms of intense stress. The silt, mud and soil block the sunlight from reaching the corals and also smother their polyps' feeding tentacles. Herbicides kill the corals' symbiotic algae, together with other plant life such as calcareous algae and seagrass beds. Pesticides enter the food chain through the animal component of the plankton and ultimately cause mortality of filter-feeding creatures and their predators by accumulating in their bodies to dangerous levels. Fertilizers and sewage contain high levels of nutrients which encourage blooms of algae to spread through the reef waters, choking the corals.

It is possible that this super-abundance of algae may trigger a plague of the herbivorous sea urchin, *Diadema*, and it also provides a source of food for the larval stage of the crown-of-thorns starfish. Both of these creatures feed on the algae, and the young crown-of-thorns starfish soon develop into coral-devouring adults. This not only leads to the death of wide areas of coral, but also reduces the success of new coral larvae settlement. With less competition from healthy or growing corals, the algae continue to flourish. Crown-of-thorns starfish and *Diadema* sea urchin infestations have been observed throughout the Indo-Pacific in regions such as the Red Sea, Mauritius, Great Barrier Reef, Moorea and Japan. The crown-of-thorns starfish is absent from the Atlantic Ocean, but during the late 1970s, *Diadema* populations exploded on Caribbean reefs (partly in response to overfishing of their natural predators such as pufferfish and triggerfish) and threatened to weaken the reefs' structure through excessive grazing before the outbreak of a natural disease epidemic in 1983 controlled their numbers.

Oil discharged from ships or land-based refineries and factories is often the most visible sign of ocean pollution. A major oil spill, such as the Persian Gulf disaster in 1990, can wreak extensive damage to coral reef ecosystems, but the continuous minor discharges that occur each day are just as lethal in the long-term. Turtles and sea cows suffocate in oil when they surface to breathe, and terns, cormorants and other sea-birds become coated in a drowning black mire as they dive for fish. Layers of tar foul turtle nesting-beaches and destroy shoreline habitats such as mangrove swamps. The corals attempt to shed the oil from their bodies by secreting copious amounts of mucus, but this requires a lot of energy. Suffocating in a chemical-laden slime, the polyps become increasingly stressed and, as a reaction, they may expel their symbiotic algae. This event is

OPPOSITE
Relics of war, such as this wrecked hull, are a reminder of conflicts in the tropical Pacific at places like Truk Lagoon and Guadalcanal.

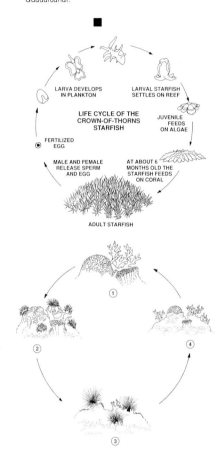

There are three main stages in the life cycle of the crown-of-thorns starfish: the release of eggs and sperm from adults leading to fertilization, the development of a free-swimming larva and the growth of a bottom-dwelling juvenile. There is probably no precise and uniform set of circumstances leading to a plague of these starfish, but a possible scenario of events giving rise to a 'crown-of-thorns cycle' could be as follows. A healthy coral reef (1) provides food for the adult starfish. The living coral tissue is eaten (2) and the starfish either migrate to find more living coral to feed on or die from starvation. Dead areas of coral are rapidly covered with algae and this may lead to a population explosion of sea urchins such as *Diadema* (3). Where the algae is grazed by the urchins, floating coral larvae have a chance to settle and begin forming new coral colonies (4). These may gradually reduce the amount of algae (leading to fewer urchins) and, in a healthy environment, the reef may return to its former balanced state (1).

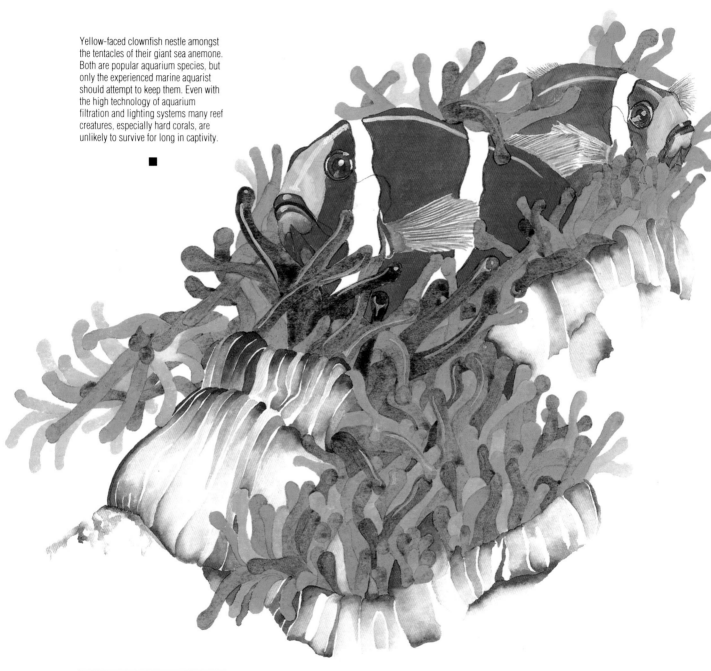

Yellow-faced clownfish nestle amongst the tentacles of their giant sea anemone. Both are popular aquarium species, but only the experienced marine aquarist should attempt to keep them. Even with the high technology of aquarium filtration and lighting systems many reef creatures, especially hard corals, are unlikely to survive for long in captivity.

■

The black pearl oyster is indigenous to French Polynesia and each year the Tuamotu Islanders dive from their outrigger canoes to harvest the valuable pearls.

known as 'bleaching', since the loss of the pigmented algal cells reduces the coral flesh to a white tone. If the causes of stress are rapidly relieved, the algae may recolonize the polyps, but prolonged bleaching causes widespread coral mortality.

Coral bleaching is not fully understood, but one of the most significant causes may be related to increases in sea-water temperature. World-wide bleaching of corals (with as much as 60% death on some Indo-Pacific reefs) has been observed since 1985. This has led to the suggestion that corals may act as 'sentinels' of climate change and reflect the current trend in global warming.

The temperature of the earth's surface has always been in

part regulated by gases, such as carbon dioxide and methane, occurring naturally in the atmosphere. Most of the heat from the sun is absorbed by the earth, but some is radiated back into the atmosphere. Here the gases trap a certain amount of the radiation and reflect it towards the planet, while the excess heat escapes into space. Thus, these gases act like the panes of glass in a greenhouse, which also inhibit the loss of heat. The denser the concentration of atmospheric 'greenhouse' gases, the greater the build-up of heat trapped above the earth's surface.

The most important greenhouse gas is carbon dioxide, which is produced as a by-product of many natural processes. Animal respiration, bush fires and decay all release carbon dioxide into the atmosphere. Approximately half of all carbon dioxide produced dissolves into the oceans where it is taken up as a raw material by marine plants and animals. On coral reefs the vast quantities of symbiotic algae inside coral polyps use the carbon dioxide to fuel their photosynthesis, while the corals themselves incorporate it into the manufacture of their limestone (calcium carbonate) skeletons. In addition, there are numerous other shell-producing creatures and marine algae on the reef and in the plankton which assimilate the carbon dioxide. Coral reefs are, therefore, extremely important as 'natural sinks' for atmospheric carbon dioxide.

Over the last two centuries, human activities have steadily been adding to the proportion of greenhouse gases in the atmosphere. Huge amounts of carbon dioxide are produced by burning fossil fuels such as coal and oil, and methane levels are rising as the domestic cattle population increases. Tropical forests are burnt (releasing more carbon dioxide) to create grasslands for the herds to graze on, and this, in turn, creates an ideal habitat for termites – another methane producer. Man-made chlorofluorocarbons (CFCs) are released in smaller quantities than either methane or carbon dioxide, but they are extremely effective greenhouse gases.

There is now broad agreement among scientists that the world may warm up by 1–2°C by the year 2030 as a result of the build up of greenhouse gases arising from industry and agriculture.

This small increase in temperature could have a significant impact on corals, and research is currently being carried out to understand how polyps and their symbiotic algae might adapt to warmer seas.

Predicted levels of global warming are also sufficient to start melting the polar ice caps. Estimates of the subsequent rise in sea level by the mid-twenty-first century vary from 0.5m to 2.0m (1.6ft to 6.6ft). Low-lying coastal regions are at threat not only

When the Second World War spilled into the Pacific Ocean, intense naval battles resulted in the sinking of dozens of ships. An entire Japanese fleet which was consigned to the sea-bed of Truk Lagoon following an American airstrike in 1944 has since been colonized by sponges and corals. The legacy of war took on a more sinister form in the Marshall Islands. Nuclear tests were started at Bikini Atoll in 1946 and reached their climax with the detonation of 'Bravo', a 15 megaton explosion which eradicated two coral cays and scattered debris from the reef over an area of 125,000 square kilometres (50,000 square miles). Radioactive fall-out was deposited on four nearby atolls, and in the years since then the incidence of cancers and deformed children has risen. The Bikini Islanders were evacuated to Kili Island 800km (500 miles) south of their devastated atoll. Today they still dream of the day when they will be able to return home, but before the relocation can take place, over a million cubic metres of radioactive topsoil will have to be scraped from the contaminated coral islands and somehow replaced.

Large industrial and commercial ports, such as Gladstone on the Queensland coast, contribute to the pollution of reef waters. Dredging channels to provide cargo ships and tankers with access to coal and oil terminals causes nutrient contamination, while the paints used on the hulls of small boats in the marinas (to stop barnacles attaching) often release toxic chemicals.

■

Charles Darwin (1809–1882) developed his Theory of Natural Selection following his return from a five-year voyage aboard HMS *Beagle*. During this epic journey of research, Darwin visited the Galapagos Islands, a rugged group of volcanic peaks straddling the equator in an isolated tract of the eastern Pacific. It was there that Darwin encountered many unique species of island life, including several subspecies of giant tortoise and an entire family of finches. Darwin's observations of these creatures led him to believe that they had slowly changed (or evolved) from ancestral stocks, developing adaptations which improved their chances of survival in certain habitats – observations that were later to be incorporated in Darwin's Theory of Evolution by Natural Selection.

from flooding, but also from storms related to upsets in global climate patterns. Intact mangrove swamps will provide a protective buffer to strong winds and waves, while healthy coral reefs will fulfil a similar role further off-shore. However, reefs will only continue to offer protection to vulnerable coastlines if they can keep pace with rising sea levels.

Research into the probable effects of a sea level rise on the Great Barrier Reef suggests a short-term beneficial response and a long-term detrimental one are likely. A potential scenario of events begins with extensive coral growth in the reef flats as these become more permanently flooded. More efficient movement of sand will nourish coral cays, allowing them to build up above the encroaching waters. However, after a prolonged period of rising seas, the maximum rates at which reefs have been known to grow upwards will be insufficient to avoid their gradual drowning. Beyond a period of a hundred years, cays will begin to disappear as water depths covering the reef flats become too great and cycles of sand distribution break down. Important sea-bird and turtle nesting sites will simply vanish and these creatures may have considerable difficulty in finding alternative locations that are as remote and undisturbed.

Other coral reefs and islands in the world may suffer from similar impacts. Island groups such as the Maldives and Tuvalu, which contribute little or nothing to the problem of global warming, are likely to be the first nations in history to drown. Along with other small island states, including Barbados, Fiji, Grenada, Mauritius, Seychelles, Tonga and Vanuatu, they have declared their intent to seek international co-operation with those industrialized countries which have overloaded the atmosphere with greenhouse gases.

Another major threat to coral reefs and islands is from a rapidly growing tourism industry. Many coral reefs occur in developing regions of the world where governments are struggling to boost economies and cope with high populations. Tourism is an ideal way of exploiting the attractiveness of reefs and islands, and for many countries in the Caribbean and tropical Indo-Pacific it now constitutes their most profitable industry. Based on an image of palm-fringed coral-sand beaches and clear blue waters, tourism promotes many reef areas as 'unspoilt' tropical paradises where visitors can escape from the stress and problems of the industrialized world. There is no reason why people should not be encouraged to enjoy the spectacular coral reef and island ecosystems at first hand, but unfortunately the rapid growth of poorly planned tourist facilities, coupled with the effectiveness of modern-day transport (in the form of jet airliners and cruise ships), has placed enormous strains on the reefs and islands.

Many of the impacts are similar to those connected with agriculture and other industries. Shoreline-protecting mangrove swamps are cleared for hotels and resorts, and pollution from sewage and desalination plants is pumped into the reef lagoons. Other forms of damage are inflicted by dredging reef flats for marinas and dynamiting channels through the reefs themselves to allow boats convenient access to beach jetties. Such activities can seriously disrupt natural patterns of water circulation between the reef-enclosed areas and the outer sea. Tides, for example, may drain with such force through a channel cut in the reef that large quantities of sand are eroded from beaches and then deposited on living corals, smothering them.

Coral cays which are developed for tourism often have little space left over for natural woodland or forest and soon lose their communities of land-birds and breeding colonies of sea-birds as a result. Many cays have been stripped of all but a few coconut palms in their conversion to island resorts complete with kitchens, restaurants, dive shops, desalination units and dozens of chalets for accommodation. Every dead leaf that falls from the remaining vegetation is swept away and burnt; apparently, leaf-litter is an 'undesirable image' to those intent on marketing paradise to the tourist. Without the recycling of nutrients from decaying plant matter, however, the cays' terrestrial ecology is effectively sterilized.

Modern forms of transport have 'shrunk' the world's oceans, enabling tourists to reach even the most remote coral islands with relative ease.

In 1972 there were only two resorts in the Maldives, but by 1989 well over seventy had been constructed.

■

The tourists themselves also damage the coral reefs and islands they visit. The coral seascapes of the reef attract hordes of snorkellers and scuba divers. Some, through inexperience, may accidentally smash a plate or branching coral with a sweep of a flipper; while others, through ignorance, may handle a coral, causing great stress to the sensitive polyps. Dive boat operators thoughtlessly toss their anchors overboard and allow them to drag across reefs, destroying, in a matter of seconds, swathes of coral that may have taken hundreds of years to mature. Recreational fishermen discard pieces of nylon fishing-line, perhaps unaware that they cause the starvation and mutilation (through entanglement) of thousands of sea-birds each year. Another danger threatens the sea-birds at their nesting colonies. Over-inquisitive tourists approach too closely and startle great clouds of them into noisy flight. Their eggs and chicks are left exposed and predatory gulls and frigatebirds swoop on them. In some areas, the size of gull populations has increased to levels beyond the natural balance of the ecosystem as a result of the rich pickings to be had from inadequate refuse disposal at island resorts or nearby rubbish dumps on the mainland. The gulls reach pest proportions and severely inhibit the breeding success of sensitive birds like the terns.

The saddest and most unnecessary aspect of the tourist industry is the associated trade in marine curios. Souvenir shops throughout the tropics are crammed with rare shells and the skeletons of corals that have often been artificially coloured with food dyes in a pathetic attempt to restore their 'living' hues. Dried starfish and turtles, shrivelled sea horses and inflated porcupine pufferfish, hanging from lengths of string, add a gruesome element to the tawdry displays.

A flourishing section of coral reef is completely devastated by a harbour-channel blasting operation.

OPPOSITE
For many people, the ultimate 'dream holiday' destination is a coral island, which conjures up an image of paradise.

■

THE IMPORTANCE OF CORAL REEFS AND ISLANDS

Human impacts to coral reefs and islands are certainly cause for great concern. A despairing and pessimistic view of the situation, however, will do nothing to ensure a brighter future for this threatened paradise. Positive and realistic action is urgently needed to safeguard it. Before conservation can gain any momentum people must be aware of the benefits it can provide and why it is necessary at all.

From an economic point of view, thriving coral reefs and their associated seagrass meadows and mangrove swamps serve as nursery grounds for fish, lobsters and prawns which later migrate to offshore waters where they are important for fishing industries. Tourism also contributes to local economies. Advocating materialistic reasons for conservation may seem contradictory, but they must be given serious consideration if

172

environmental problems are to be solved in a realistic manner.

Reefs still harbour species yet to be identified and, like the tropical rainforests, they are important reservoirs of biological diversity. As the one species on earth with the power to control the fate of all the others, it is our moral obligation to conserve the incredible wealth of life on this planet. Islands are of special importance since they contain endemic species found nowhere else.

Coral reefs and islands are also essential for educational and scientific purposes. They make excellent natural laboratories where fundamental aspects of biology, such as evolution, can be studied. By understanding the ecology of natural islands, we should be in a better position to reflect upon the impact of reducing other world ecosystems such as rainforests, grasslands and moorlands to 'islands in a sea of human development'.

Modern scientific research is currently being carried out to identify reef creatures that may be of use in anti-cancer and anti-AIDS screening. Some of the sedentary inhabitants of the reef prevent other animals from growing over them by secreting special chemicals, and these could play a role in the production of antibiotics. Several species have already been found to contain substances which block ultraviolet radiation and biologists are investigating ways of making artificial copies for use in suncare preparations.

Furthermore, coral reefs and mangrove swamps help prevent shoreline erosion and protect highly populated coastal regions from tidal waves and strong storms.

The importance of conserving coral reef and island ecosystems is clear. The challenge is *how* to conserve them for the benefit of not only the threatened species and rich and diverse habitats they contain, but also for other reasons such as scientific research, public education, fisheries and tourism.

SAFEGUARDING FOR THE FUTURE

Before any kind of effective conservation can be implemented a detailed understanding of how the ecosystem works is essential. Surveys of coral reefs and islands must be carried out in order to accumulate information on the types of habitats, plants and animals that are present and how they interact with each other. Points of special interest and importance such as rare endemic island species, turtle nesting sites, sea cow feeding grounds, land and sea-bird breeding colonies and reef fish nursery areas build up an overall picture of the ecosystem. Several organizations world-wide, including the Smithsonian Institution, International Union for the Conservation of Nature (IUCN), World Wide Fund for Nature and the Australian Institute for Marine Science,

OPPOSITE
Observations of roosting silver gulls reveal a number of behavioural postures. In this field sketch, one gull is stretching and another is asleep. A pair of gulls are facing each other in a dramatic and noisy two-stage display. This begins with an arched and aggressive posture and switches rapidly to one that suggests appeasement.

Recording the various species of bird along with their feeding and roosting habitat requirements is an important aspect of conservation planning. This field sketch is part of a five-week census recording the arrival of migratory waders to Heron Island on the Great Barrier Reef.

A sad reflection of a modern throw-away society. Oceans have become the dumping grounds for everything, from highly toxic waste to empty plastic bottles. Each year, numerous turtles face a needless death by choking on discarded plastic bags which they mistake for edible jellyfish.

collect an enormous quantity of information each year. The Tropical Marine Research Unit at the University of York (England) is well-known for its Reefwatch project which enables any diver or snorkeller to contribute to our growing knowledge of coral reefs.

A lot of this research activity can also be channelled into assessing and monitoring human impacts, since understanding the problems facing the environment is the second major step towards conservation. The Tropical Marine Research Unit, for example, has investigated several aspects of human pressure including the impact of sand and coral mining in Mauritius, the effects of oil spills in the Red Sea and the development of tourism in the West Indies.

Equipped with an extensive database, scientists and conservationists are able to help governments and local communities become more aware of the need to protect their natural resources, and can co-operate with them to work out the most appropriate conservation strategy. Throughout the world, this has led to many forms of positive conservation action.

In the Maldives, for example, the government-operated Marine Research Section has launched a scheme known as 'Adopt a Coral'. The resort staff on tourist islands, and members of local communities on other inhabited islands, are asked to identify and adopt a *Porites* coral and a table coral, which thrive on their reefs. Each month the corals are checked for any signs of damage: the table corals are particularly vulnerable to physical stress from divers, whereas the deterioration of the *Porites* corals, which may be several hundred years old, may suggest a chronic impact such as severe pollution. Thus, the scheme not only helps to monitor the health of the marine environment, but also stimulates environmental awareness amongst Maldivians and tourists.

Other schemes in the Maldives include sampling reef fish catches (to determine the impact of fishing) and monitoring populations of the crown-of-thorns starfish. Tuna are only allowed to be caught using traditional pole-and-line methods in place of the large drift-nets which claim the lives of dolphins and turtles. There is, without doubt, an eagerness in the Maldives to implement conservation-based projects, but this beautiful nation of coral reefs and islands still has many environmental problems. Rubbish and sewage continue to be tipped on reefs, tourism is overloading certain atolls, and large volumes of sand and coral are mined each year.

Innovative technology has a vital role to play in alleviating or even eliminating some of these stresses. The development of the permanent mooring buoy, for example, prevents tourist boats from causing anchor damage to reefs. An eye-bolt is drilled into a

Mangrove clearance not only obliterates a diverse community of plants and animals, but also renders the shoreline vulnerable to erosion.

Hawksbill turtles nest on the beaches of the Suakin Islands in the Red Sea between March and July. As far back as 2,000 years ago, traders regarded their shells as highly prized commodities.

small bare section of the reef, away from living corals, and attached to a surface buoy by a length of rope. Boats can simply be secured to the buoy, so there is no need for an anchor to be thrown overboard. New sewage collection and disposal systems are being designed for island resorts to reduce effluent discharge onto their reefs.

On a global scale, it is of paramount importance to develop more efficient and cleaner forms of energy in order to curb man-made greenhouse gas emissions, and thereby attempt to resolve the problems of climate change and sea level rise which threaten not only coral reefs and islands, but a whole range of world habitats.

International legislation and conservation already help to control activities such as the trade in marine curios. The Convention on International Trade in Endangered Species of Wild Fauna and Flora (CITES) is a treaty of over 110 countries, including Britain and the United States of America, which have imposed strict laws on the import and export of rare and threatened species. CITES prohibits all international commercial trade in marine turtles and carefully regulates trade in clams and most varieties of coral.

Very little is known about many of the species collected for the curio trade. The distribution and abundance of molluscs such as conch, triton, abalone, cowry, nautilus and helmet shells is difficult to assess since many are nocturnal and well camouflaged. Predicting the impact of their collection is, therefore, extremely complicated. Nevertheless, scientists are continuously studying these creatures with a view to understanding more about their life histories and the potential for using artificially cultured juveniles to replenish depleted populations. It is possible that some species could be harvested on a sustainable basis, and attempts are now being made to farm the giant clam (for both its meat and shell) in many Pacific countries including the Republic of the Marshall Islands.

To conserve a population of an endangered species in the wild it helps if their habitat is also protected. The Hawaiian Islands National Wildlife Refuge provides a sanctuary for the world's last remaining population of Hawaiian monk seals. Dedicated scientists carefully monitor their numbers by tagging recently born seal pups. Orphaned pups are airlifted to the Sea Life Park at Honolulu where they are hand-reared before being reintroduced to the wild. Monk seals are extremely sensitive to disturbance, particularly while nursing their pups on beaches, and human activity on the refuge's coral islands is strictly limited to research purposes. This type of exclusive preservation is easily achieved in the uninhabited and remote Hawaiian Leeward

For sale: dried, stuffed turtles set in glaze-eyed rigormortis with brittle flippers spread in crucifixion. All international trade in marine turtles is prohibited since all eight species are listed as endangered, but *local exploitation* is still permitted in some countries and causes the deaths of many turtles each year. Those tourists who want more than the vivid memories of their reef experience should consider purchasing a photograph of a healthy reef rather than taking home one of its dead inhabitants.

■

Islands, but how does conservation work in more accessible locations which are frequented by humans?

The World Wide Fund for Nature (WWF) plays a significant role in the protection of the earth's fauna and flora. One of its recent projects (in association with IUCN and the South Pacific Regional Environment Programme) has been centred on the raised reef islands of Palau in Micronesia. The so-called 'Seventy Rock Islands' were established as a wildlife reserve in the mid-1950s and are particularly important for their populations of rare species such as the Micronesian megapode, the Palau scops owl and an endemic palm. Hawksbill and green turtles nest on the beaches, while in the surrounding waters dugongs and coral reefs thrive. Field-work has enabled scientists to create a plan which will not only help to control illegal dynamite fishing and poaching, but will also provide future protection for the reserve and its inhabitants and determine its potential for research, education and carefully regulated tourism. The plan for Palau's Rock Islands incorporates the theme of *conservation management*.

Management plans help to ensure the sustainable use of the resources of reefs and islands while maintaining the beauty and diversity of their environments. Managing protected coral reefs and islands in this manner is now widely accepted as an effective and realistic approach to conservation.

The largest protected area of coral reefs in the world is the Great Barrier Reef Marine Park. Many of its associated coral cays and continental islands are protected as national parks. The marine park was established in 1975 following an outcry from the Australian public over proposals to drill the reef for oil. In 1981, the reef was inscribed on the World Heritage List as a region of outstanding beauty and natural importance. It also meets the requirements for classification as a biosphere reserve – a representative sample of a major ecosystem.

The Great Barrier Reef Marine Park Authority successfully manages the reef through a zonation system. Preservation zones prohibit all human activity with the exception of strictly controlled scientific research. Marine National Park zones can mainly be used for scientific, educational and recreational purposes, while the remaining zones are for general use, including commercial fishing. The system effectively separates activities which conflict or compete with one another and all zones are continually monitored by scientists to ensure that natural resources can be sustained indefinitely. Permits, entrance fees and other forms of income generated by the marine park are balanced against the costs of managing the environment, staffing (in the form of a team of park rangers) and

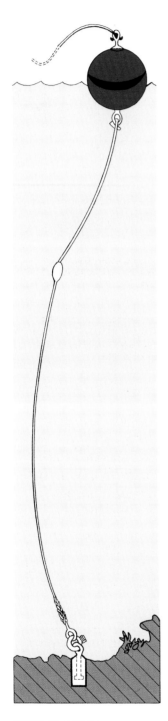

Permanent mooring buoy.

providing educational facilities.

On Heron Island, in the Capricorn Group of the Great Barrier Reef, rangers from the Queensland National Parks and Wildlife Service monitor the annual arrival of nesting turtles and also operate a tourist visitor centre which displays various environmental themes. Such research and education are essential elements in the ongoing struggle to conserve the world's coral reefs and islands.

The international importance of coral reefs and islands is recognized by numerous organizations, such as Earthwatch and the Marine Conservation Society, which continue to increase world-wide public awareness of conservation issues.

There is always the danger, however, that our greed will destroy whole habitats before conservation programmes have been properly implemented. Conservation stems from scientific knowledge. The slow development of protected parks, closely coupled with scientific programmes which support their conservation, must never be outpaced by commercialism if coral reefs and islands are to remain a paradise.

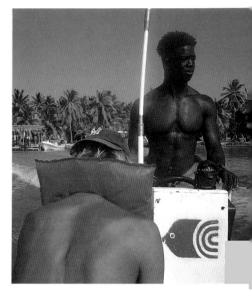

Coral Cay Conservation has a well-equipped field headquarters on South Water Cay, a coral island on the Belize Barrier Reef. Ray Roland, shown here coxing one of its dive boats, is a Belizean keen to promote a greater awareness amongst his local community of the importance of preserving this unique ecosystem.

■

CONSERVATION IN ACTION

Packed with an array of scuba tanks, buoyancy jackets, weight belts and other diving gear, one of Coral Cay Conservation's fast, open dive boats is ready for action. The divers, volunteers from many countries around the world, clamber aboard. They are followed by a dive master and a boat cox, making the full complement for this particular survey trip eight people. Once cast off, the dive boat drifts away from the purpose-built jetty on South Water Cay, the Coral Cay Conservation headquarters on the Belize Barrier Reef. Tiny sergeant-major damselfish dart amongst more sedate sea horses which cling to the algae growing on the submerged stilts of the jetty. The dive boat's powerful outboard engine, gurgling in neutral, suddenly roars as the boat cox engages the throttle. The bow lifts slightly in eager response and the boat accelerates away from the coral cay.

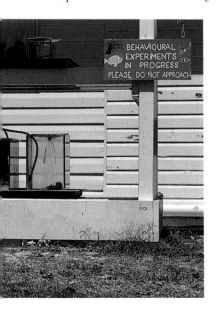

A white reef heron puzzles over an unattainable source of fish. The Heron Island Research Station, operated by the University of Queensland, provides outstanding opportunities and facilities for visiting students and scientists.

■

Swinging out of the shallow, protected lagoon area with its meadows of seagrass and isolated patch reefs, and then looping round towards deeper water, the diving team passes through a natural gap in the spectacular barrier reef formation between South Water and Carrie Bow Cays. The dive boat turns north, skipping over the waves of open sea that roll past and then collapse in white foam on the barrier reef crest. A computerized on-board satellite navigation system plots the boat's progress, and with accuracy the cox guides the boat towards the dive site. The engine idles once more, and a depth reading is taken to confirm the boat's position. A lone magnificent frigatebird soars

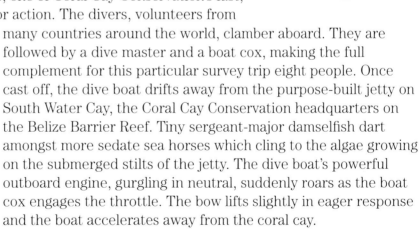

This false colour satellite image (Landsat TM Thematic Mapper, March 1991) shows the southern-most reaches of the Belize Barrier Reef and depicts an area of 450 square kilometres (174 square miles). The barrier reef platform is clearly visible as a narrow red band curving to form a distinctive hook shape. The tiny green dots surrounded by yellow areas on the barrier reef are the Sapodilla Cays. A particularly interesting feature of this image is the group of thin red lines radiating from the tip of the barrier reef. This unusual pattern of coral growth is believed to mirror the ancient embankments of a river delta that existed there during the Ice Age when a lowering of sea levels had uncovered the continental shelf. Although the prehistoric delta was drowned about 7,000 years ago when rising sea levels signalled the end of the Ice Age, its position has been faithfully recorded by coral growth. As well as highlighting features such as this, which are often impossible to detect by divers, satellite imagery plays an important role in conservation monitoring and mapping. *(Reproduced by permission of Earth Observation Satellite Company, Lanham, Maryland, USA)*

■

The United Nations Environment Programme has now established a set of guidelines for the aquarium trade to help improve the collection process and to ensure that it is properly managed on a sustainable basis. Some countries are banning the import of certain species and introducing labelling systems which will advise inexperienced aquarists as to the suitability of various species.

overhead on rapier wings, twisting its head from side to side to peer down at the divers as they clamber into their diving gear, fastening scuba tanks to their backs.

The tropical Caribbean sun makes the fully-clad divers uncomfortably hot and they are eager to enter the water. As soon as safety checks have been carried out, they manoeuvre into a sitting position on the sides of the boat; two rows of divers facing each other. The dive master gives the signal, and each diver somersaults backwards into the sea. Six goggled faces soon reappear at the surface, give the 'all is well' sign to the dive master, and then slowly descend beneath the waves.

The divers operate in pairs, swimming along a pre-arranged survey transect. Slowly finning a few metres above the reef, they record several pieces of information in special waterproof notebooks: the topography of the seascape, the different habitats, the varieties and abundance of fish, algae, sponges, corals and other invertebrates, and any signs of natural or human impact. One diver navigates using a compass, while another tows a surface buoy to enable the dive master in the boat to check the survey team's position.

Many of the divers who join Coral Cay Conservation's unique expeditions arrive as novices with little open-water experience. After a period of one to three months diving, however, they are not only extremely proficient in their technique, but have also

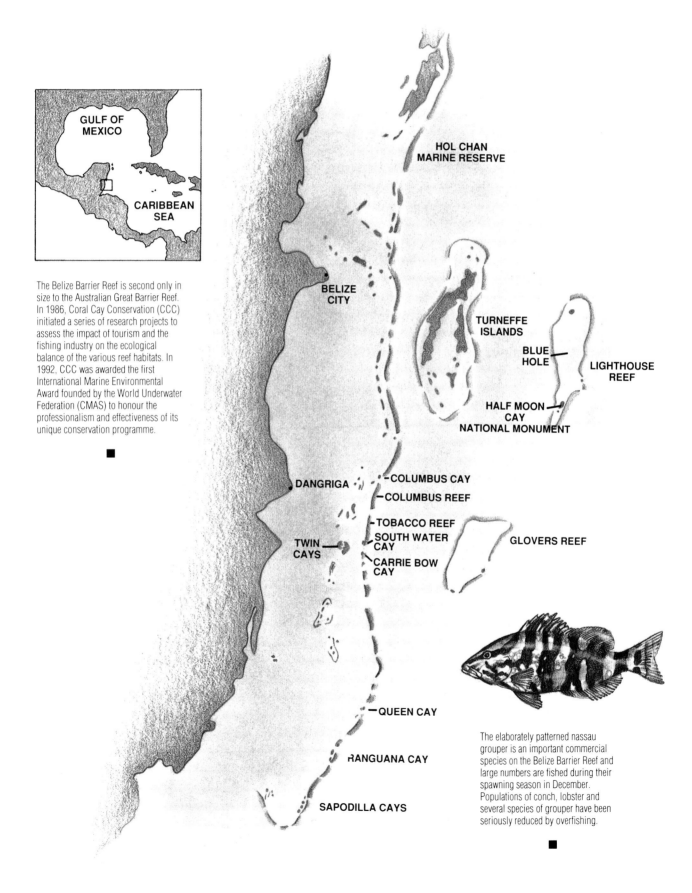

GULF OF
MEXICO

CARIBBEAN
SEA

The Belize Barrier Reef is second only in size to the Australian Great Barrier Reef. In 1986, Coral Cay Conservation (CCC) initiated a series of research projects to assess the impact of tourism and the fishing industry on the ecological balance of the various reef habitats. In 1992, CCC was awarded the first International Marine Environmental Award founded by the World Underwater Federation (CMAS) to honour the professionalism and effectiveness of its unique conservation programme.

■

HOL CHAN
MARINE RESERVE

BELIZE
CITY

TURNEFFE
ISLANDS

BLUE
HOLE

LIGHTHOUSE
REEF

HALF MOON
CAY
NATIONAL MONUMENT

DANGRIGA

COLUMBUS CAY

COLUMBUS REEF

TOBACCO REEF
SOUTH WATER
CAY

GLOVERS REEF

TWIN
CAYS

CARRIE BOW
CAY

QUEEN CAY

RANGUANA CAY

SAPODILLA CAYS

The elaborately patterned nassau grouper is an important commercial species on the Belize Barrier Reef and large numbers are fished during their spawning season in December. Populations of conch, lobster and several species of grouper have been seriously reduced by overfishing.

■

learned a great deal about the coral reef ecosystem – both from their own observations and with the guidance of expert marine scientists who work with the Coral Cay Conservation teams.

The six divers are approaching the end of their survey as they reach the crest of the steep outer drop-off which plummets for hundreds of metres to the ocean floor. Here it is not uncommon for the divers to have a close encounter with curious eagle rays or glimpse the fleeting shape of a wary grey reef shark. Each dive adds a new dimension to their experience of this fascinating and beautiful ecosystem.

The Belize Barrier Reef, the second largest in the world and described by the United Nations Environment Programme as 'unique in the western hemisphere on account of its size, its array of reef types and the luxuriance of corals thriving in such pristine condition', is now threatened by rapidly increasing tourism as well as destructive industrial and agricultural development. The Belize Government is aware of the need to implement conservation management programmes for the protection of the barrier reef and has already established the Hol Chan Marine Reserve and the Half Moon Cay Natural Monument

A Coral Cay Conservation diver carefully secures the rope of a surface buoy to mark the position of a future survey-dive site.

ABOVE RIGHT
A coral island in the Sapodilla Group, Belize Barrier Reef.

■

in conjunction with non-governmental organizations, such as the Belize Audubon Society and the Belize Centre for Environmental Studies. Similar reserves are urgently required in the southern sections of the reef before they become despoiled by poorly managed tourism. Coral Cay Conservation, as an independent, non-profit-making organization, has been asked by the Belize Government to establish the country's second marine reserve at South Water Cay.

The divers surface and haul themselves back into the dive boat. Animated discussions recount the memorable moments of the dive as the team journeys back towards South Water Cay. The information it has recorded will form a small but vital part of the extensive database being compiled by Coral Cay Conservation. This will be used in conjunction with satellite images to create and monitor a management scheme for the new marine reserve.

Coral Cay Conservation is also sending expeditionary teams of divers and field-workers to the Sapodilla Cays to begin surveying the pristine coral reefs and islands in that remote southern section of the Belize Barrier Reef.

'The palm tree grows, the coral spreads, but man shall vanish.'
(A POLYNESIAN SAYING)

AFTERWORD

A percentage of this book's royalties are being donated to the following organizations to assist with their important research and conservation work on coral reefs and islands.

Coral Cay Conservation (UK) is working with the government and people of Belize to establish marine reserves and devise management plans for the protection of the Belize Barrier Reef. Royalties will help to fund a programme of survey work around the Sapodilla Cays.

NYZS The Wildlife Conservation Society (USA) supports coral reef field research in Belize and Kenya. In 1990, the Society purchased Middle Cay, a small coral island at Glovers Reef Atoll, with a view to creating a ranger and research station. In Kenya, the Society supports research into the impact of fishing on Indian Ocean coral reefs. In 1992, the Society launched its Coral Reef Conservation Initiative, a major programme of research, management and education, which includes the founding of a reef studies unit at the Society's New York Aquarium. A donation from this book's royalties will contribute to the Coral Reef Conservation Initiative.

The Great Barrier Reef Marine Park Authority (Australia) 'provides for the protection, wise use, understanding and enjoyment of the Great Barrier Reef in perpetuity through the development and care of the Park'. Royalties from this book will help to fund an educational display at the Authority's Great Barrier Reef Aquarium in Townsville.

I have been lucky enough to witness the truly unique and stunning spectacle of many coral reefs and islands throughout the world, and through this book I hope I have shown you some of that beauty. Most of all, however, I hope I have portrayed an image of a paradise that you will wish to treasure, respect and conserve.

WILLIAM GRAY

GLOSSARY

ALGAE
A large group of mainly aquatic plants, ranging from microscopic single-celled plankton to large seaweeds. Many forms on a coral reef are described as *calcareous*, being able to deposit calcium carbonate (or lime) in their tissues.

ALGAL RIM
A smooth compacted rocky pavement built by calcareous algae on the most highly exposed, wave-battered region of a coral reef. A term used to describe Pacific reefs.

AMPHIPOD
An aquatic crustacean which usually has a laterally compressed body.

ATOLL
A ring-shaped coral reef enclosing a central lagoon.

BARRIER REEF
A coral reef separated from the coast by a channel that is too deep for coral growth.

BEACH ROCK
A dark ridge of hard rock found on the beaches of some coral islands, formed by the chemical cementation of sand grains.

BLEACHING
A term used to describe the expulsion of symbiotic algae from corals that are under stress.

BIVALVES
Molluscs that have a shell with two parts (or valves) hinged together, such as the clams.

BRYOZOANS
Small, colonial marine animals often forming brightly coloured moss-like growths.

BUDDING
A form of asexual reproduction found in invertebrates, in which a new individual grows out of a parent one.

CAY
An island formed by the accumulation of sand and rubble on top of a coral reef.

CONTINENTAL DRIFT
A theory which has led to the conclusion that the continents are in continual motion over the earth's surface.

CONTINENTAL SHELF
The relatively flat margin of a continent, forming a shallow sea between the coastline and the continental slope.

COPEPODS
A group of generally microscopic marine crustaceans found in plankton.

COPRA
The dried flesh (or kernel) of the coconut, from which coconut oil is pressed. The residue is used as animal feed.

CRUSTACEANS
A large group of hard-shelled animals including the crabs, lobsters, prawns and barnacles.

ECHOLOCATION
A system of orientation used by cave swiftlets, whales, dolphins and some bats, in which a series of high-frequency clicks is emitted. The returning echoes are used to determine the presence of nearby obstacles or prey.

ECOSYSTEM
The ecological system in which a community of living things interact with each other and with their physical, non-living environment, and in which nutrients are effectively recycled.

ENDEMISM
A plant or animal species confined to a particular region, such as an isolated island.

FORAMINIFERANS
Single-celled, planktonic animals that secrete hard shells of lime.

FRINGING REEF
A coral reef growing on the shoreline of an island or other landmass.

GASTROPODS
Molluscs that usually possess a single coiled, conical or flat shell including abalones, limpets, winkles and conches.

GUANO
Sea-bird excrement, which in large accumulations is valuable as a natural fertilizer. It contains high levels of nitrogen, phosphorus and potassium.

HOT SPOT
A concentrated area of molten rock (magma) beneath the earth's crust, usually associated with volcanic eruptions.

MICRO-ATOLL
A coral colony (usually of *Porites*) growing in the shallow water of the reef flat which is prevented from growing above the level of low tide, and therefore assumes a plateau shape.

MID-OCEAN RIDGE
A region of intense volcanic activity, leading to the creation of new ocean crust and fuelling the process of sea floor spreading.

MOLLUSCS
A large group of invertebrate animals which includes the chitons, gastropods, bivalves and octopus.

NUDIBRANCHS
A family of slug-like gastropods in which the shell has been lost; the gills are exposed as feathery tufts.

PARASITE
An organism which obtains nourishment from the tissues of another organism.

PATCH REEF
A patch of corals growing on the sandy floor of the reef flat or lagoon.

PHOTOSYNTHESIS
The process by which plants use sunlight to convert carbon dioxide and water to carbohydrate, with the formation of oxygen as a by-product.

PLANKTON
A collection of very small animals (zooplankton) and plants (phytoplankton) which float or drift in the water for all or part of their lives.

PLANT SUCCESSION
The process of vegetation change over a

length of time, initiated by the colonization of pioneer species.

PLANULA
The free-floating larval stage of a coral.

POLYP
A simple animal consisting of a tubular body opening into a mouth surrounded by a ring of tentacles. Coral colonies are made up of numerous interconnected polyps.

RHIZOME
A stem which grows underground.

SEAMOUNT
A submarine mountain; usually of volcanic origin.

SEA SQUIRT
A group of colonial or solitary animals (also known as ascidians) which filter sea-water through their bodies.

SYMBIOSIS
Two unrelated individuals living together and both benefitting from each other's presence.

ZOOXANTHELLAE
Algae which live in symbiosis with many corals, some clams and a few other varieties of reef animal.

USEFUL ADDRESSES

CORAL CAY
CONSERVATION
The Sutton Business
Centre
Restmor Way
Wallington
Surrey SME 7AH, UK

The Coral Cay
Conservation Programme
provides volunteers with
a unique opportunity to
join major diving
expeditions, based on
remote coral islands, to
help conserve the Belize
Barrier Reef.

The following
organizations are all
directly involved with the
conservation and study
of coral reefs, coral
islands or a combination
of the two.

AUSTRALIAN
INSTITUTE FOR
MARINE SCIENCE
Caper Ferguson PMB 3
Townsville
Queensland 4810
Australia

CENTRE FOR MARINE
CONSERVATION
1725 DeSales Street, N.W.
Washington 20036
USA

COUSTEAU SOCIETY
870 Greenbrier Circle
Suite 402
Chesapeake
Virginia 23320
USA

GLOBAL CORAL REEF
ALLIANCE
324 North Bedford Road
Chappaqua
New York
NY 10514
USA

EARTHWATCH
(HEADQUARTERS)
680 Mount Auburn
Street
PO Box 403
Watertown
MA 02272-9104, USA

EARTHWATCH
(EUROPE)
Belsyre Court
57 Woodstock Road
Oxford
OX2 6HU, UK

EARTHWATCH
(AUSTRALIA)
PO Box C360
Clarence Street
Sydney 2000,
Australia

FAUNA AND FLORA
PRESERVATION
SOCIETY
1 Kensington Gore
London SW7 2AR, UK

GREAT BARRIER REEF
MARINE PARK
AUTHORITY
1–37 Flinders Street East
PO Box 1379
Townsville
Queensland 4810,
Australia

GREENPEACE
AUSTRALIA
Studio 14
37 Nicholson Street
Balmain, NSW 2041
AUSTRALIA

GREENPEACE UK
30–31 Islington Green
London N1 8XE, UK

GREENPEACE USA
1436 U Street NW
Washington DC 20009
USA

INTERNATIONAL
COUNCIL FOR BIRD
PRESERVATION
32 Cambridge Road
Girton
Cambridge CB3 0BJ, UK

INTERNATIONAL
UNION FOR THE
CONSERVATION OF
NATURE
Avenue de Mont Blanc
1196 Gland
Switzerland

MARINE
CONSERVATION
SOCIETY
9 Gloucester Road
Ross-on-Wye
Herefordshire HR9 5BU,
UK

NATURE
CONSERVANCY, THE
Pacific Regional Office
1116 Smith Street
#201 Honolulu
Hawaii 96817, USA

NYZS THE WILDLIFE
CONSERVATION
SOCIETY
Bronx
NY 10460, USA

REEF RELIEF
PO BOX 430
Key West
Florida 33041–0430
USA

SMITHSONIAN
INSTITUTION
National Museum of
Natural History
Washington DC 20560
USA

TROPICAL MARINE
RESEARCH UNIT
(REEFWATCH
PROJECT)
Department of Biology
University of York
York YO1 5DD, UK

WHALE AND DOLPHIN
CONSERVATION
SOCIETY
19A James Street West
Bath
Avon BA1 2BT, UK

WORLD
CONSERVATION
MONITORING CENTRE
219c Huntingdon Road
Cambridge CB3 0DL, UK

WWF (WORLD WIDE
FUND FOR NATURE)
Panda House
Weyside Park
Godalming
Surrey GU7 1XR, UK

WWF
(INTERNATIONAL)
Avenue de Mont Blanc
1196 Gland
Switzerland

BIBLIOGRAPHY

*Atlantic Barrier Reef
Ecosystem at Carrie
Bow Cay, Belize, The,*
Rutzler and Macintyre
(ed), Smithsonian
Institution Press, 1982

*Australia and the South
Pacific*, K. Deacon,
Simon Schuster, 1989

Barrier Reef Traveller,
David and Carolyn
Colfelt, Windward
Publications Pty Ltd,
1989

BBC Wildlife Magazine
(various editions),
British Broadcasting
Corporation

Belize Barrier Reef Ecosystem, The, Judith S. Perkins, New York Zoological Society Report, 1983

Beyond the Reefs – Shark for Sale (Adventures in the Seychelles), William Travis, Arrow Books Ltd, 1990

Biology and Geology of Coral Reefs Volume III, 'The Birds of the Great Barrier Reef', Professor J. Kikkawa, Academic Press Inc, 1976

Birds of the Seychelles and the Outlying Islands, The, Malcolm Penny, Collins, 1974

Common Reef Fishes of the Maldives, Charles Anderson and Ahamed Hafiz, Novelty Press, 1987 (part 1), 1989 (part 2)

Coral Island, A – The Story of One Tree Island and its Reef, Harold Heatwole, Collins, 1981

Coral Reef Directory, The – Coral Reefs of the World, Volumes I, II and III, Sue Wells (ed), IUCN Conservation Monitoring Centre, 1988

Coral Reef Fishes of the Indian and Western Pacific Oceans, A Field Guide to the, R.H. Carcasson, Collins, 1977

Coral Reef Handbook, The, The Australian Coral Reef Society

Coral Reefs, Les Holliday, Salamander Books Ltd, 1989

Corals of the World, Dr E. Wood, t.f.h.

Publications, 1983

Crown of Thorns (COT) Newsletter (various editions), Marine Research Section, Ministry of Fisheries and Agriculture, The Republic of Maldives

Exploring Australia's Great Barrier Reef – A World Heritage Site, Lester Cannon and Mark Coyen, The Watermark Press, 1990

Fishes of the Caribbean Reefs, I. Took, Macmillan Education Ltd, 1990

Fragile Paradise, A – Nature and Man in the Pacific, Andrew Mitchell, Collins, 1989

Great Barrier Reef, Reader's Digest Book of the, Reader's Digest Association (Sydney), 1984

Great Barrier Reef, The, Allan Power, Summit Books, 1980

Great Barrier Reef Area, A Protected Seascape, G. Kelleher, R. Childs, P. Quilty, Great Barrier Reef Marine Park Authority, 1989

Kon-Tiki Expedition, The, Thor Heyerdahl, George Allen and Unwin Ltd, 1953

Life and Death in a Coral Sea, Jacques-Yves Cousteau, Cassell, 1971

Life on Earth, David Attenborough, Collins BBC Books, 1979

Light in the Sea, David Doubilet, Swan Hill Press, 1989

Living Planet, The,

David Attenborough, Collins BBC Books, 1984

Living World, The, Professor B. Cox, Dr P.D. Moore, Dr P. Whitfield, David Attenborough, Marshall Editions Ltd, 1989

Lost Paradise – The Exploration of the Pacific, Ian Cameron, Century, 1987

Mafia Island Marine Park Project, Gudrun Gaudian and Matt Richmond, The People's Trust for Endangered Species, 1990

Maldives – A Nation of Islands, Department of Tourism (Republic of Maldives), Media Transasia Ltd, 1983

Marine Curio Trade, The, Sue Wells and Elizabeth Wood, Marine Conservation Society, 1991

Marine Plants of the Caribbean, D. Littler, M. Littler, K. Bucher, J. Norris, Airlife Publishing Ltd, 1989

National Geographic Magazine (various editions), National Geographic Society

Natural History of the Coral Reef, A, Charles R.C. Sheppard, Blandford, 1983

Oceans and Islands – The Encyclopedia of the Earth, Dr Frank H. Talbot, Dr Robert E. Stevenson, Merehurst Ltd, 1991

'People Pressures on the Reef' in *Reeflections,* No. 26, Great Barrier Reef Marine Park Authority,

September 1991

Projected Research and Development Activities 1991/1996, Australian Institute of Marine Science, 1991

Red Sea, The, Dr P. Vine, Immel Publishing, 1985

Reef – A Safari through the Coral World, J. Deitsch Stafford, Headline, 1991

Reef Creatures Identification (Florida, Caribbean, Bahamas), Paul Humann, New World Publications Inc, 1991

Reef Fish Identification (Florida, Caribbean, Bahamas), Paul Humann, New World Publications Inc, 1991

Save the Earth, Jonathon Porritt, Dorling Kindersley Ltd, 1991

Seabirds – An Identification Guide, Peter Harrison, Croom Helm Ltd, 1983

Story of the Earth, The, Geological Museum (London), 1972

Study of One Tree Island, Great Barrier Reef, Australia, H. Heatwole; T. Done, E. Cameron, Dr W. Junk Publishers, 1981

Trials of Life, The, David Attenborough, Collins BBC Books, 1990

Voyage of the Beagle, Charles Darwin, Penguin Books, 1989

World's Wild Shores, The, National Geographic Society, 1990

INDEX